Pastor Mike,
I pray this
book is a b...
to you and your
church!

James Moore
John 8:12

The Light Switch

James Moore

E ergreen
PRESS
Mobile, Alabama

Evergreen Press
P.O. Box 191540 • Mobile, AL 36619
800-367-8203

Contents

Acknowledgments

In 2009, God inspired *The Light Switch* when He told me to look at evangelism another way. He showed me that my personal experiences and training could make a huge impact on the Kingdom of God by showing Christians that they have an opportunity and responsibility to make a difference in an extraordinary way. I have included many true stories about winning unbelievers to the Lord by stepping into their lives with the Gospel and making an impact.

The Lord led me through every step of the writing of this book by providing creative and unique ways to convey His message to the church. He also gave me some phenomenal opportunities to win souls along the way. The theme and title for *The Light Switch* were developed on a Thursday night in 2010, as I prepared to share a short devotional at our church's choir practice. God showed me that most of the world is stumbling around in the dark and needs someone with a light to lead them to the light switch named Jesus Christ.

During the five years this book has been in the making, I attended Bible school and seminary and wrote a thesis on personal evangelism, which served as my primary research for this book. This has been a unique and fulfilling experience in which many acknowledgments are due. First, the Lord deserves all the credit for the things He has accomplished in me over the last almost fifteen years of my walk with Him. Second only to Him have been the contributions and encouragement of my wife, Melissa, who led me to the Lord in the first place and has been by my side through the journey. My precious daughters, Elise and Avonlea, have sacrificed time with Dad as they watched me type away and research for this work.

My mother, Ina, and my brothers, Chris, Nate, Mike, and Marc, have been a great encouragement and have always believed in my ministry. I would like to thank Benita Vasiloff for editing the first draft of this book, and Charles Hefton, Steve Curry, Sara Curry, Jerry and Jan Bradley, and my mother for proofreading and editing the final draft. Last, but not least, thank you to my thesis working group, who made my evangelism experiment possible. Jodie and Michelle Ryan, Jaime and Josh Bowser, Jean Gingrich, Erik Fraticelli, Janel Weaver, Michelle Georgiev, Jordan Drake, and Briana Williams—thank you!

Preface

I once read a short fishing story called "Emlyn and the Far Pools."* It went something like this:

"I wish there were more," Emlyn said to his family as he brought his fish catch into the house. After all, the whole village depended on fish. Even the landlord required the citizens to catch sufficient fish for the market. Only then would their town grow and prosper.

The fish pools supplied the needs of the village. They stretched up the valley, almost as far as you could see. Those nearest were right on the edge of the village, set in comfortable fields with pleasant shade. Go farther away, though, and you came to rocky pools with steep sides and limited access. Farthest of all, up against the dark forest, were the murky pools where you had to watch for quicksand. Insects were a real problem there. Numerous beasts of prey lived in the forest, so it was best not to fish alone. Emlyn had been there occasionally.

In theory, everyone in the village was meant to go fishing regularly and even carry a small net when outside, in case they found themselves near a pool. They held regular meetings and discussion clubs about fishing, and the library contained many fishing books. Most villagers loved to hear the old stories about fishing exploits in past years, especially from the pools near the dark forest. But only a few villagers went fishing regularly. Most people were too busy with activities within the village itself.

It was relatively easy to fish in the ponds near the village. Access was simple, the fish would take the bait, and they were usually docile when caught. The problem was that the bait didn't work so well in ponds farther away. Occasionally someone suggested experimenting with different bait, but many villagers opposed this, calling it an unnatural compromise in the art of fishing. The village shop sold only standard bait anyway. The few people who had success in the far ponds were those who had taken time to understand the lifestyle of the fish there. They spent some of their time not fishing at all, but wading up to their waists in the water—watching, learning, and relating to the fish.

And those fish from the distant ponds! They got a good price at the market but often looked strange and unfamiliar to the villagers. They flopped wildly when caught, stinging the unsuspecting fisher with their spines. The ones living in ponds near the dark forest seemed the strangest of all, with their unusual shapes and behavior. Poisonous too, some of the villagers believed. Yet they fetched a good price in the market, which was operated on a co-operative basis by the landlord. Indeed, he seemed to welcome these different fish as much as any.

Emlyn knew that the ponds near the village, though not fished out, were getting sparse. The village could never grow if it depended on these alone. "I must go farther out," he said. "Experiment with bait. Find out what they like. Take precautions against the stinging spines. Maybe work in a small team." And he did.

And this is what James Moore does every day of his life, completely dedicated to the Great Cause of the Great Commission, to go into all the world and make followers of Jesus Christ.

In almost thirty years of ministry, I've never met a person with more passion and zeal for winning the lost to Christ. I've also never met anyone with more success and effectiveness. The methods James uses and teaches simply work. His unique and proven techniques have equipped many believers and continue to bear fruit.

Rooted in scripture and grounded in love, the book you are about to read will help every believer and every church to become an effective and strong witness for Christ. Get ready to become a great witness for Jesus Christ!

Stephen Curry
Senior Pastor, Foothills Assembly of God
Fort Collins, CO

*http://www.internetevangelismday.com/fishing.php. Used by permission.

Introduction

Does a light burn bright and hot within you—with seemingly no way to shine? Do you have a blazing desire to do more for God but don't know what He is calling you to do? Do you sense the Lord building something within you, but you fear you don't have what it takes to accomplish it? These are normal feelings for people of God who desire to be difference-makers for His Kingdom. I can relate to those feelings. I have, at times, thought I was going to burst if I didn't have a chance to impact my little world around me for God in some great way.

God is calling us to make the extraordinary the ordinary by seeing what He has set before each of us and making a choice to act on it in the moments of uncertainty. He will meet us there with great power and results. Each of us has been given a ministry to reach the lost in our small area of life—our family, friends, neighbors, coworkers, and those we meet by chance. Behind each of those doors is an inspiring and wonderful story of redemption just waiting to be written. You have been given a great gift: the light of Jesus. You can make a great difference in the darkness of the world, right where you are, with your abilities and resources.

All around us, people are desperately hurting, confused, and utterly without hope. They rely on us to bring a message of love and comfort through our relationship with our Lord. They look to us but don't admit it. They wait and linger, wondering if we will make an impact on them. They are drawn to the light but are uncertain of its source. Those people need our testimony, even in a small way, of the Lord's faithfulness and power to meet their needs in the pit they're in.

The answer is simple: start somewhere. Even if your somewhere is only a small impact on a life through a simple act of love or service, start somewhere. God will meet you there in a mighty way. He will bless you for taking a step to further His Kingdom.

If your light is burning brighter than you can contain, you have been given enough to help light the way for another. God is working in you. He believes in you. And He desires to work through you and fulfill your burning desire to make a difference. I pray you will find the encouragement you need through the journey called *The Light Switch*.

1

Impacting the World

For many years I have considered it my personal ministry to evangelize those in my daily life and point them toward Christ. Over time I felt a calling to make my ministry official and to lead Christians into *their* calling as mighty witnesses for Christ. I attended Bible school and seminary and am now an evangelist and teacher dedicated to inspiring churches and leaders to reignite the Church's passion for the lost. I continue to share the Gospel with anyone and everyone I encounter and disciple those I have won to the ways of Christ.

When God first found me and saved me, I had no idea all the places I would go—to Afghanistan where I was part of a counter-terrorism force searching for Osama bin Laden, to Texas where I led an undercover drug operation, to Washington where I was assigned to guard important dignitaries—and all the people I would come across and lead to Him. I am no one special. I am just willing to make a difference for God by making an impact on the world around me for Him.

Going back to the beginning of my walk with God, in January 1998, I married a wonderful Christian girl named Melissa. I had already been in the Army for two years and had just returned from a deployment to Bosnia. After spending the last nine months of my Germany tour with my new wife, we were reassigned to Fort Hood, Texas, where I agreed to start attending church with Melissa.

When we landed at a little church in the town of Copperas Cove, I had to adjust to spending every Sunday in church, but I pressed through it and continued. One Sunday night, we had a guest evangelist named Gary Richards who preached a wonderful message and then gave an altar call by asking us all, "If you died tonight, where would you go?"

With tears in my eyes, I admitted to my wife, "I wouldn't make it." That night, I made a decision to give my life to Jesus, and I have never looked back.

I was so delighted with my new life that I had to share it with others. I could hardly contain my zeal. About that time, God began to promote me. Out of about one thousand military policemen on Fort Hood, I was chosen to be one of the eight members of the Special Reaction Team. This was essentially the Army's version of a SWAT team. I was quickly promoted to sergeant over all my peers and led the daily operations of the team for about eighteen months. At that time I applied to the Army's Criminal Investigation Division (CID) and was quickly accepted. After helping to resolve a major hostage situation we were involved in, I said goodbye to the team to start my new career as a special agent.

A New Career

Upon completion of the grueling four-month CID school, I was sworn in as a special agent, and they presented me with my gold badge and credentials. This was a very big day in my life. At age twenty-three, I was a sergeant, a special agent, a criminal investigator, the husband of a wonderful woman, and most importantly, a child of the living God!

At this point, I knew a little bit of the Bible, had been a little churched, and lived a pretty good life. I wanted to make a difference in the lives of those around me, so I began calling my brothers and sharing my testimony with them, as well as with my co-workers. I didn't feel quite adequate in my knowledge of the Word or in my level of "righteousness," but I shared what I knew and touched people's lives within my capabilities.

In my new career as a special agent, I was a tenacious investigator, not wanting a single case to slip through the cracks unsolved. I worked extremely hard and solved some big cases. During my first couple years, I investigated dozens of deaths, countless rapes, arsons, and every type of felony you can imagine. I was having an action-packed time loving my job, but I also saw my position as a great opportunity to serve God. I spent my days with grieving parents, battered victims, broken lives, and hopeless felons. I used the broken and hopeless moments of these victims, witnesses, and suspects as an avenue into their hearts. Of course every suspect I apprehended was first read his rights and interrogated.

I almost always ended up with a signed confession, which

is essentially a ticket to prison in a felony investigation. You would think each of my suspects went away to prison with no hope, since that was the normal process. However, this child of God was not going to let an opportunity like that pass by. After every interrogation, I always took off my badge and set it on the table. I then informed the suspect that he was no longer talking with Special Agent Moore but with a fellow man who cared about his soul.

I sometimes spent two hours sharing the Gospel of Jesus Christ with someone who had just confessed to a horrible crime. I showed them mercy and not judgment, and after sharing the Gospel, I always gave the person an opportunity to accept Christ. Not only were many good cases solved, but also many souls were won to the Lord during those times. Most of my suspects would shake my hand, cry, and hug me before they were transported off to years behind bars.

I also took many opportunities to share the Gospel with grieving parents of deceased children, families of murder victims, and witnesses to horrific crimes. My fellow agents knew what I was doing but never resisted the work of God. On the contrary, some of their lives were touched by merely eavesdropping on my conversations with my suspects. This was a season of much fruit for the Kingdom of God.

With each person I witnessed to, I became a better soul winner. I continued in the Word and grew in my understanding and ability to witness effectively and make an impact on those around me. God honored me again because I had been honoring Him. I was promoted to staff sergeant while I was still twenty-three years old. I had become a seasoned and accredited investigator.

Searching for Osama bin Laden

Shortly after 9-11, I was selected to be a member of a counter-terrorism task force working alongside the FBI. This was a huge moment for me. I was the youngest member of the task force and rapidly deployed to Afghanistan. I spent most of my days climbing the Hindu Cush Mountains, searching caves, and taking DNA samples and fingerprints from dead Al-Qaeda members. Our ultimate goal was to find Osama bin Laden.

While not in the mountains, I spent my days in the US camps in Kandahar and Bagram. I used this time to grow in the Word and do some fine-tuning in the Lord. While others in my tent watched dirty movies on their laptop computers, I read the Bible and attended chapel services. I sang in the Kandahar Choir, which was a small group that sang for our outdoor church services in the courtyard of the former Kandahar Airport every Sunday. I worked hard and served the Lord with all my heart.

God saved me from many close calls, including a hard landing in a helicopter with my buddy Shem, but most of all by guarding my heart in a godless place. In March, 2002, we mounted a major offensive, called Operation Anaconda, against the Taliban and Al-Qaeda in the high-mountain regions of central and eastern Afghanistan. I was a DNA and forensics expert tasked to collect and exploit information that would lead to the capture of the top terrorists, notably bin Laden.

During Operation Anaconda, I investigated a combat crime scene on what is infamously known as Roberts Ridge. This was named after Petty Officer Neil Roberts, a US Navy Seal who was killed on that hilltop just a few days before. On one of my missions in Operation Anaconda, I happened to be patrolling a valley with the 10th Mountain Division when one of their soldiers slipped and fell down the side of the steep mountain.

The soldier was a staff sergeant who injured his leg badly when he fell. He couldn't move and was in a vulnerable position if we would begin to take fire. So I stripped off my gear and left it and my weapon with my partner, Kevin. I ran to the injured man and examined his lower leg. It had a compound fracture.

"Do you trust me?" I asked him.

"Yes, I trust you."

As I picked up the man and cradled him in my arms, he kept assuring me that he would return to fight and apologizing for his injury. I carried the soldier down the mountain and to a safe landing zone for a helicopter, which was waiting there with one skid on the side of the mountain as we arrived. At that point, I climbed back to the top, gathered my gear, and continued the mission, not thinking twice about what had just happened. I was proud of the injured man for having the desire to return.

One week before we left Afghanistan, I was heartbroken that I hadn't found Osama bin Laden because I had planned to share the Gospel with him if we captured him. I was picturing myself in the mountains witnessing to him when we received a mission to fly to a remote mountain region near Tora Bora to find some bodies. This was the place of the last sighting of Osama, and we searched until we found some al-Qaeda graves on a large pinnacle on the edge of a great river. I helped dig up twenty-three graves of al-Qaeda fighters. From them I obtained and documented DNA samples and personally transported them to Washington, DC, for release to the FBI lab.

A Hero's Welcome

This was not the only reason we had to return home through Washington, DC. We all assumed that the CID commanding general wanted to parade us around as his first soldiers to return from the War on Terror. On Monday, we were told to report to the CID headquarters for a ceremony. Anxious to get this over with so we could return to our families, we arrived at the headquarters building. They had an award ceremony planned, and a crowd of guests attended. As I stood with those with whom I had just deployed, the commanding general arrived and conducted a pinning ceremony. The host of the ceremony read each award citation, and the Army Commendation Medal was pinned on all of them, but I was still left.

Then the host announced, "Attention to Orders" again. He read the citation as, "By order of the President of the

United States" and awarded me the Bronze Star Medal for rescuing that man in the mountains. My heart went out to each of my comrades because I felt unworthy of that honor if they didn't receive it too.

I later discovered this was one of the first Bronze Star Medals issued in the War on Terror. You see, God honored me because I had honored Him. This isn't about me. This is not the part of the book where I tell you how cool or decorated I am. This is about the Lord. He takes care of His children.

Upon returning to Fort Hood, Texas, I felt like a small celebrity. The news channels interviewed me coming off the plane, my name was printed in the newspapers, and my face was on the evening news. God was promoting me because I was willing to serve Him.

When I returned to work, the special agent in charge of the CID office asked me to lead the Undercover Drug operation. I willingly accepted the challenge. I was put in charge of a team and given plenty of funds and resources to get the bad guys. After the apprehension, searches, and legal stuff, I shared the Gospel with them. Again, much fruit was borne during this time as I made the most of each opportunity given me to witness to drug dealers.

Guarding Dignitaries

In 2003, I was reassigned to a different type of mission. I was given orders from the Pentagon to become a member of the Department of Defense Protective Services Unit (PSU). At first, I wasn't excited about guarding dignitaries, but God had a great plan. The day I arrived in the summer of 2003, I received a phone call from a friend back at Fort Hood, who told me I'd been promoted to sergeant first class, or E-7. I was assigned to the Metro Protection Detail for Secretary of Defense Donald Rumsfeld. I again found myself in an interesting situation and a highly visible position.

After a few months on residence watch, I was promoted to the motorcade detail where several other agents and I transported the Secretary to and from the Pentagon, the White House, Capitol Hill, and other distinguished venues around the beltway. Given that this was the first wave of the War in Iraq, you can imagine how many times a week we were at the West Wing or taking "Rummy" (as we referred to him) to the halls of Congress to testify before the House and Senate Armed Services Committees.

The West Wing trips served as an excellent opportunity to get each of my family members a box of official White House M&Ms. During the waiting times, while in the bowels of the Pentagon or in the motorcade, I took advantage of the opportunity to talk to my fellow agents about the Lord.

After a few months working within the beltway, my leadership selected me to be a member of the Travel Team. I was reassigned to the highest mobile travel team, which was the Joint Chiefs of Staff. This was when my mission trips began. Basically the team's job was to make advance trips to the country the Chairman of the Joint Chiefs of Staff planned to visit. We made all security arrangements with the host nation's Secret Service equivalent, wired the hotel for security, and served as the protection detail when the boss (as we referred to any protectee) arrived.

After my very first trip, I was promoted to the position of Mission Special Agent-in-Charge. Now I was the senior man responsible for the security of the highest-ranking general in the United States military, General Richard Myers. My schedule was unbelievable. I went to the Super Bowl, spent time with celebrities, and conducted joint missions with the Secret Service to protect President Bush and many of his cabinet.

My wife is the most understanding woman for sticking with me through all this. I would fly out of Dulles, conduct a mission somewhere for two weeks, go directly to a different region for another week, then fly home for two days and back on the road again. Sometimes I had only a few hours to see my wife. I traveled to just about every region in the world, from Colombia to Japan to Latvia to Iraq.

I took advantage of these trips as opportunities to spread the Gospel. I witnessed to airplane seatmates, hotel workers, drivers, baggage workers, and anyone else I met during my travels. I was a missionary funded by the federal government. I took the Gospel to the uttermost parts of the earth and bore much fruit for the Kingdom of God. I witnessed to my fellow agents as well, and many seeds were planted. I was beginning to be very good at what I did best—soul winning. I also took this opportunity to impact the lives of my little brothers, nieces, and nephews by getting them each a souvenir from every country I was in.

In January 2005, I was selected to be the operations sergeant for the entire unit. It didn't take me long to figure out a way to advance the Kingdom of God through my position. One of my responsibilities was to coordinate the arrival of all newly assigned agents and their families. What an opportunity! I took my job a step further and ensured that these incoming agents and their families were taken care of far beyond the obligations that came with my job.

My family and I picked them up from the airport and oriented them to the area while we helped them get to their hotel. Then, if they had any pets, we housed them at our place until they could get settled in their new homes. If they had household items, we allowed them to store them in our garage so they could turn in their moving truck and save money. We helped some agents find a home, some find a job, and some we just became friends with. Our impact on the Protective Services Unit was maximized by our willingness to step into the lives of others and do what we could with what we were given.

Into the Limo

At the end of 2005, I was selected to be the personal security officer (PSO) to the Deputy Secretary of Defense. That meant I was the close-in bodyguard and personal liaison to the second in command of all US Armed Forces. I served

Secretary England and spent a great deal of time with him. As part of a dynamic team of agents, I helped protect him wherever he traveled (to the Pentagon, the White House, dinners at ambassadors' homes, on fly-fishing trips, and even at his home). As the PSO, I also had a more personal relationship with him. I spent a lot of time with him in addition to the other operations. I rode in the limo with him, worked out at the Pentagon Athletic Club with him, and flew with him when he traveled.

Protecting dignitaries was just one more amazing opportunity to share the Gospel with people all over the world. Once God provided an opportunity for me to share my faith with a dignitary I was protecting. I do not think it would be appropriate to mention this person's name, but I will share the basics of our conversation. While riding with the boss one day, after some small talk, he made the comment that all roads lead to the same God. First I wondered if it were my place to share my faith with one of the most powerful men in our government, but I went for it. I respectfully but confidently disagreed. "There is only one way to God, and that is Jesus Christ."

I told him that Jesus is "the way and the truth and the life" (John 14:6), and no one could get to God except through Him. I didn't know this man's faith background and still don't, but I shared my faith anyway. I told him that Jesus Christ had changed my life.

He looked at me as if to say, "You are pretty bold, young man," but I held my ground and he graciously received the message. I could have lost my job that day, but he was in danger of losing his soul. I had to speak up on God's behalf.

In early 2006, I began my application process with the FBI. It was a job I had dreamed of since I was sixteen. I was coming to the end of my enlistment so, after ten years, I was leaving the Army for the FBI, or so I thought.

God began doing something different in me. My buddy Neal, who had already been accepted by the bureau, called and asked if I were still going to join the bureau with him. I had to disappoint Neal as I informed him of my heart change. I no longer thought I was supposed to join the FBI. I was not ready because God was stirring something else in me. I had no idea what it was.

Needing a job, I was recruited by a government contracting firm to conduct interrogations for the US Army's military intelligence. Even though I was a former special agent with CID, the Army still required me to go through the joint interrogation certification course. When I went to this course, God began showing me the blueprint for this book, and that was when I knew I was going to write. God was showing me that I needed to equip others in the Christian world to win souls, using the methods I had been using for years.

I began writing this book as I deployed to Iraq to interrogate terrorists and insurgents. I arrived in Baghdad and immediately began conducting interrogations of Iraqi prisoners, but my soul-winning days continued. I spent the first few weeks fighting some of the most intense spiritual warfare I had ever faced. The enemy of our souls knew I was going to make a great impact and tried to stop me, but I persevered.

Within days, I began winning souls. Whether it was on the basketball court, in the chow hall, or in the camp, I was making an impact for the Lord. I even shared the Gospel with an insurgent I was interrogating. God did awesome things, and I was able to lead many soldiers and civilians to the Lord and reach an entire combat community with the Gospel.

My purpose for sharing these experiences is for you to see the impact one person can make for the Kingdom of God. As I look back over the last fifteen years, I imagine there are hundreds of people now serving God because of my testimony and personal impact on their lives. It also excites me to think about how many hundreds of people they impacted with their testimonies.

Do you see the possibilities when someone is willing to accept their general calling to spread the Gospel? If I can go all over the world and make the most of so many opportunities to win souls, then rest assured you can do the same in your effort to reach your neighbor, co-worker, family member, or friend. Just as you have read how I made an impact on the world around me for Him, I look forward to hearing of the mighty exploits you will do for the Lord!

2

In the Beginning

Now let us turn to your mission. I would be remiss if I didn't immediately challenge you to accept and begin to fulfill your mission to bring God's light to the friends, relatives, and neighbors whom you know and the other people you come across in your everyday life.

Whether you continue your walk with God as a minister to those around you or feel called to embark on an official ministry, you are a minister. You are a leader to those who are lost. You are a vital asset to the Kingdom of God and I pray your zeal for souls, coupled with the power of God, will fuel your evangelistic endeavors. You need to never forget your calling to pull people from the fire by sharing with them the same light that God has given to you.

In the beginning God created the heavens and the earth. Now the earth was formless and empty, darkness was over the surface of the deep, and the Spirit of God was hovering over the waters. And God said, "Let there be light," and there was light (Genesis 1:1-3).

Let's further discuss this light that God wants you to share with others. When God created the world, He said, "'Let there be light,' and there was light" (Genesis 1:3). When He turned on the lights in the world by His spoken Word, it was not merely physical light that entered the world but also Himself. The Bible states that "God is light; in him there is no darkness at all" (1 John 1:5b).

Since He is the source of all light, He shattered the darkness with His presence. At that time, sin was nonexistent, so this world was an acceptable place for Him to dwell as He walked in the garden in the cool of the day. When Adam and Eve disobeyed and stepped into darkness, they fell from the grace and presence of God, and He withdrew Himself from the world.

The world retained its physical light but was immediately thrust into a great expanse of spiritual darkness. Because of the loss of God's glorious presence, mankind's nature changed to sinfulness, and God turned out the lights. He could never again dwell there as He had, because light can have no fellowship with darkness.

Yet God still longed to restore fellowship with His creation. To accomplish this, He installed a light switch in every person. This light switch is Jesus Christ. God would never again turn on the lights in this world without someone making a choice. Jesus came into this world to be the light of the world but could dwell in a person's life only by their decision to turn on the light switch.

Upon His departure from this world, God alluded to this

plan when He declared, "'I will put enmity between you and the woman and between your offspring and hers; he will crush your head, and you will strike His heel'" (Genesis 3:15). The devil, who had stolen God's people from His presence, would not have the ultimate victory. He would only bruise Christ, but Christ would crush his head, once and for all, later on the cross.

The fall of man was a great heartbreak to God, but it was not a surprise to Him because Christ was "chosen before the creation of the world" (1 Peter 1:20a). God knew that true love required a choice. He would not force anyone to love or serve Him, but He let them choose between obedience and rebellion. God knew that people would eventually act upon their temptation, so He installed the light switch long before the lights went out. He loves us so much that He provided the plan for a second chance before He gave us our first. In fact, Christ was present during the creation of the world and knew that one day He would rescue it from darkness after the lights went out. As John wrote,

In the beginning was the Word, and the Word was with God, and the Word was God. He was with God in the beginning. Through him all things were made; without him nothing was made that has been made. In him was life, and that life was the light of all mankind. The light shines in the darkness, and the darkness has not overcome it (John 1:1-5).

While He was involved in creating us, He knew He would have to die for us, yet He did not change His plan. He created a people that He knew would break His heart, and for them He would allow Satan to bruise His heel. He did this because He loves us.

At a time when the world was in utter darkness and depravity, the Father gave the command for the light to enter the world. He knew His mission would end in humility, so He arrived under humble circumstances. He came as both God and man and shared in our humanity so He could be the perfect advocate for us before the Father. He was able to sympathize with our weaknesses because He too took on flesh and was "tempted in every way, just as we are—yet was without sin" (Hebrews 4:15). Darkness had no effect on Him because He was pure light and came with a mission to shatter the darkness.

He hoped that all would receive Him. But the faithful witness, John, wrote, "He was in the world, and though the world was made through him, the world did not recognize him" (John 1:10). Many darkened hearts would not see Him as the light. Rather, they took advantage of His humility and tried to overcome Him. He walked among them and waited for the moment the Father had ordained for Him to conquer the darkness through what seemed like defeat. He willingly went to the cross and, while we were still sinners, He died for us. He crushed Satan's head on the cross in the moment of redemption. The light seemed extinguished, but He rose again and shined His light into our hearts. He remains the light of the world but, sadly, much of the world remains in darkness because they have not turned on the light switch.

I am the light of the world; he that follows me will never walk in darkness but have the light of life (John 8:12).

This light switch is not simply a fixture installed on the wall of humanity but represents a choice to *switch* from darkness to light; from evil to good; from rebellion to obedience. When Jesus appeared to Saul, later known as the Apostle Paul, He gave him this mission:

I am sending you to them to open their eyes and turn them from darkness to light, and from the power of Satan to God, so that they may receive forgiveness of sins and a place among those who are sanctified by faith in me (Acts 26:17-18).

The Dark Room

The following is a parable that may help further explain about God's light switch.

Many people lived in a certain large house in a dark place with each of its many rooms being the home of a different person. An old man lived in a dark room at the end of a long hallway where no one else had gone for years. This man had spent his existence in total darkness. His body was covered with scars from the wounds he received as he stumbled over the obstacles in his room. He had heard there was a light switch somewhere in the room, but he had lost interest in finding it because he was no longer convinced there was a power source connected to it.

All the other rooms in the house were occupied except one. Some occupants stumbled around their rooms in darkness, just like the old man. Some had a light, but it had flickered so long that they felt more comfortable in the darkness and questioned the need for the light. Some had a bright light, but they kept their doors closed. These were content with their light and did not stumble, fall, or walk in the darkness, but their light was of no value to anyone else in the house. Some had found the light and decided to crack their door so others could share their light if they happened upon it.

One day, a new man moved in to occupy the empty room. This man brought a light with him and was convinced of its power source. He left his door open at all times and frequently took his light with him throughout the house to assist those in darkness and save them from falling. One night the new man shined his light down the dark hallway and discovered a secluded entrance to a room he'd never visited. He immediately went to the door and opened it, shining his light into the room. An old man sat in a chair in the middle of the room, surrounded on all sides by dangerous obstacles.

The new man's light was so bright, the old man could hardly open his eyes at first. But as he squinted through the light, he began to make out the objects closest to him. His eyes soon began to adapt, and he could see all the things that had cluttered his room for so long. He then saw a reflection of himself and was amazed because he had always pictured himself differently.

20

Then the new man led the old man through the obstacles to the light switch. The new man implored him to turn on the light because soon he and his light would be gone, and the old man would need a light of his own.

He hesitated because he was still not convinced he needed a light, and he continued to question the power source itself. But through the testimony of the new man, he regained hope. The new man said he once walked in darkness too, but someone with a light led him to the light switch, and he chose to turn it on. Most importantly, he told the old man that he knew the power source to be Faithful and True. Because of his confidence in the light and his desire to help others find it, the old man turned on the light switch, and his world was illuminated. For the first time in his life, he realized there is no true state of darkness, only the absence of light.

Is Your Light On?

When you read the above story, which situation did you best identify with? Are you like the old man who had become friends with the darkness? This man did not know God and was living in the old life before Christ was invited in to make all things new. The old man represents most of the world, stumbling in the darkness over the obstacles there. This could not describe someone who follows Christ, since the Word of God is a lamp for the feet and a light for the Christians' path to keep them from stumbling in darkness like the old man. In His famous Sermon on the Mount, Jesus said,

Enter through the narrow gate. For wide is the gate and broad is the road that leads to destruction, and many enter through it. But small is the gate and narrow the road that leads to life, and only a few find it (Matthew 7:13).

This clearly states that most of the world is walking on a southbound road toward death, symbolic of eternal separation from God. This describes the spiritual condition of those we need to lead to the light switch, not of those doing the leading. If this group characterizes you spiritually, you will have a difficult time leading anyone to Jesus, as you have nothing to light the way. That would be like the blind leading the blind.

Many times when a blind person was mentioned in scripture, that person had a deeper spiritual issue than merely his physical inability to see. We are spiritually blind before Christ opens our eyes. Hence the lyrics to the classic song "Amazing Grace"—"I once was blind, but now I see." As Christ said when referring to the Pharisees, "Leave them; they are blind guides. If a blind man leads a blind man, both will fall into a pit" (Matthew 15:14). We all know that the Pharisees were not physically blind, but rather unable to see spiritually.

Christ was referring to anyone who does not know God but attempts to be a spiritual guide for another. My goal is not to discourage you, but to show you that if you are not walking with God but you attempt to lead another, you could cause some damage.

But there's a simple fix for that. By your willingness to pick up this book, you've shown that you have a desire to know God. You can be a soul winner, but first, let's consider your heart condition. Yes, you have a heart condition; everyone does. What is the condition of your heart? Is it ready to receive Christ? Becoming a follower of Christ is laying down your life in full surrender, making Him both Savior and Lord. By so doing, you commit your life, will, future, and desires to Jesus, and you decide to trust and obey Him in all things.

Are you ready to surrender? I would encourage you not to wait. The Apostle Paul saw the urgency of the matter and described your *today* like this: "I tell you, *now* is the time of God's favor, *now* is the day of salvation" (2 Corinthians 6:2). Don't wait! Remember, the Kingdom of God needs you as much as you need it. Imagine the many souls that could be counting on your testimony for their hope in Christ. My prayer is that you would not go another day or attempt to lead anyone until you have made a decision for Jesus. And if this is your moment of salvation, welcome to the family of God. Now, get ready to win souls as God helps you and as you read on.

Is Your Light Flickering?

Do you identify with the occupants whose lights were flickering? These are the folks who have had an experience with God but have allowed the world to corrupt and distract them, robbing them of their spiritual relationship. Many in the church today probably identify with this condition. I don't say that in judgment, but rather through observation. People in this condition desperately need to re-consecrate their temple (themselves) and find revival in the heart of God. On a large scale, this group corresponds to the Church of Laodicea in Revelation 3:15-17, which I believe represents a spiritual condition, but also specifically represents the church of the end times. Let's read:

> *I know your deeds, that you are neither cold nor hot. I wish you were either one or the other! So, because you are lukewarm—neither cold nor hot—I am about to spit you out of my mouth. You say, 'I am rich; I have acquired wealth and do not need a thing.' But you do not realize that you are wretched, pitiful, poor, blind and naked.*

Notice this doesn't refer to physical poverty, blindness, or nakedness, but rather their lack of heavenly reward, their spiritual blindness, and their exposed flesh without a robe of righteousness. You may go to church or have chosen Christianity to be the religion you identify with. You may have asked Christ to be your Savior, but not your Lord. He must be both. If your light is flickering, you need the Master Electrician. If you make the effort to put in a work order for a new power supply, I guarantee you that He will complete it free of charge. Only then will you be ready to lead others to the light switch. Flickering lights don't provide unbelievers with the confidence they need in order to make a decision for Christ. They want to see that you are certain of the power source behind the light switch.

Is Your Door Closed?

Maybe you identified with those who had a bright light

but were reluctant to share it with others. First, if you identify with this group, you deserve a big round of applause for your faithfulness to serve God with your life. God called and you answered! You seem to have gotten the salvation part right, and that is great. Now you need to stretch yourself into your general calling as a follower of Christ. Every believer has a specific calling and gifting in a particular area, but we all have a general calling to witness for the one who hung on a cross for us. Consider the following scripture and let it speak to your heart, not in judgment, just as a wakeup call.

Again, it will be like a man going on a journey, who called his servants and entrusted his property to them. To one he gave five talents of money, to another two talents, and to another one talent, each according to his ability (Matthew 25:14).

Christ was not using the parable of the talents to teach us economic principles, but to teach us to use what we have been given and multiply it for the Kingdom of God, according to our ability. The servant with a lot of ability was entrusted with a lot of the Master's possessions, but he was expected to multiply it equally as much. The man with a moderate level of ability was given a moderate level of responsibility and was expected to multiply it. The one with little ability was given little responsibility but was still expected to multiply it.

How does this equate to evangelism? Well, not all Christians are given equal soul-winning abilities. Some are more outgoing, some are moderate minglers, and some are just sweet-spirited, quiet believers. All of the above are okay because that is how the Master made us. The Master will not expect you to do what you are not capable of. But if you don't feel particularly gifted in witnessing, please don't think you are off the hook.

Continuing with the parable, Jesus said that the servant who was given five talents gained another five. He was given much and multiplied it equally as much. The servant who was given two talents gained two more, according to his ability. But the one-talent servant dug a hole and buried it, accomplishing nothing. This servant was the only one to whom Christ declared, "'You wicked, lazy servant!'" (Matthew 25:26a). But to the two who had accomplished the Lord's mission, He gave the same commendation and reward: "'Well done, good and faithful servant! You have been faithful with a few things; I will put you in charge of many things. Come and share your master's happiness!'" (verses 21, 23).

It is interesting to note that both of these good servants received the same reward, even though their increase differed greatly. The master was happy with them because, according to their abilities, they multiplied what they had been given. But the master's final response to the lazy servant was, "And throw that worthless servant outside, into the darkness, where there will be weeping and gnashing of teeth'" (verse 30).

This is not simply about the unbelievers who will be lost if you fail to share the Gospel. You also could stand in judgment without the benefit of Christ standing with you. After all, Christ's advocacy on your behalf is dependent upon your advocacy of Him on earth. How do I know this? Well, if the lazy servant's judgment wasn't enough to convince you, let's look at Jesus' words in Matthew 10:32:

> *Whoever acknowledges me before men, I will also acknowledge him before my Father in heaven. But whoever disowns me before men, I will disown him before my Father in heaven.*

I believe that most of the time, people with great evangelism abilities recognize their gifting in reaching the lost, and so do those around them. Many of them go into ministry. But those who have only a low or moderate gift of evangelism don't understand that they are called to evangelize, even though they are not especially gifted to do so. As a result, they leave all evangelism to those who are especially gifted to reach the lost. But we must consider the value of a single talent, which weighed over 130 pounds. Imagine the value of 130 pounds of gold today, when one ounce of gold is sold for almost one thousand dollars.

Believers who fail to share their faith because they don't feel they have much to share need to consider that the Master has still entrusted them with a great deal of His treasure. Another thing to consider is the great value the treasure will have to an unbeliever in spiritual poverty. Your message, no matter how poor its delivery, is a pot of gold to those who are spiritually poor and a feast to those begging for spiritual bread.

Shine your light within your capabilities, but for those things you cannot control, trust God. Some of the greatest evangelists and teachers recognize that God's power starts working when theirs runs out. Consider Paul's words:

> *But he said to me, "My grace is sufficient for you, for my power is made perfect in weakness." Therefore I will boast all the more gladly about my weaknesses, so that Christ's power may rest on me* (2 Corinthians 12:9).

Do what God has enabled you to do, and see what he can do through you. This is an act of faith. Taking the first step to share your faith may be frightening to you, but God will carry you through it if you are obedient.

Outgoing Christians who don't have a problem sharing their faith may have another area that needs improvement. Maybe your zeal level is high, but your understanding of the Word is low. Whatever your ability, just recognize that we all have weaknesses and areas that can use improvement. You must be willing to stretch yourself when it is time.

Remember that the light that has been placed in you is God's. This is not your light to do with as you like. God lit the candle so it could shine before men. The servant who buried what the master gave him is similar to the man who was given a light and put it under a basket. Neither took the opportunity to benefit anyone else with what they were given. We need to pray and ask God to rewire our light switch. Then we need to understand that shining our light is not just someone else's job. It's a shared burden throughout the church.

You may think sharing Christ is somebody else's responsibility—the pastor, evangelist, missionary, or street preacher. But pastors can't do it all! They are to equip you to do the work of God in your daily lives. Neither the pastor nor the evangelist works where you work, and they don't share your neighbors, family, or acquaintances. This life is not just for our enjoyment. This is an area of reality that the church needs to embrace and either get on board with what God requires or miss the train.

Unfortunately, most of the church identifies with this condition when it comes to evangelism. Lifeway Research conducted a study, and they found that 80 percent of Christians surveyed believe they have a personal responsibility to share their faith with non-believers. But only 25 percent shared their faith once or twice in the past six months, and even fewer (14 percent) shared their faith three or more times in the last six months. These numbers are staggeringly low and show the desperate condition of most of the church.

Don't feel as if you have to have all the answers right now. Instead, focus on becoming willing to be a witness once you are equipped. If you want to know how to put your willingness into action, keep reading. This book, along with the power of the Holy Spirit, will help you tear down the walls of timidity and equip you to be who you were called to be—a soul-winner.

Are You Actively Seeking Those in the Dark?

And finally, some of you may have identified most with the man who took his light throughout the house and shared it with those in darkness. My inspiration for the illustration, *The Dark Room*, came from Christ's words in many scriptures like the following:

> *You are the light of the world. A city on a hill cannot be hidden. Neither do people light a lamp and put it under a bowl. Instead they put it on its stand, and it gives light to everyone in the house* (Matthew 5:14-15).

If you identify most with this spiritual condition, you are among the faithful and willing who have found the power source but also want to lead others to the light switch. I pray that you will become a more effective soul winner through this journey of *The Light Switch*.

3

Ambassadors

As you begin to discover your personal mission field, be purposeful in your actions to seek the lost. Pray about your mission field that God will open doors for you into the hearts of those who are in need of the Gospel. Let the Spirit guide you. Listen as He puts someone on your heart, prepares their heart for your message, and leads you to and through the encounter. In this chapter I am going to show you how you are called to be an ambassador for God.

The Diplomatic World

My first embassy experience with an ambassador opened my eyes to the diplomatic world in a whole new way. One of my responsibilities as a Mission Special Agent-in-Charge (MSAC) was to coordinate all my logistical, operational, and communications needs though the US Embassy, which always served as our host.

One thing I learned early on while working at the US Embassy was that the embassy grounds are internationally recognized as the sovereign territory of the United States. That meant I was walking on US soil halfway around the world. Technically, I was home.

Another thing I learned was that the original name for an American embassy in a foreign country was a *mission*, and the ambassador is still referred to as the Chief of Mission. I then discovered something much more astounding than this. The ambassador is considered the president of the United States while he is in his assigned country. He speaks on behalf of the president, but more amazingly, he does so thousands of miles away.

The president's situation is quite restrictive, as he cannot live on foreign soil but must reside in the homeland and trust that his representatives are doing his bidding on foreign soil. An ambassador, on the other hand, is the lead diplomatic official to a foreign country and conducts meetings and liaisons with the highest foreign officials on behalf of the president. This position is one of the highest honors that can be bestowed upon an individual, but it also comes with a grand responsibility. The ambassador has a proactive job. The relations between the United States of America and a foreign country are strategic and vital to our national interest and, in many cases, to our national security.

The ambassador is the president's eyes and ears on the ground, conveying his intent to foreign heads of state. If the ambassador is negligent in his duties, an international diplomatic catastrophe could occur. He must know the foreign officials, persuade them to accept the policies and decisions of the United States and, in some cases, facilitate the reconciliation of a broken relationship.

Ambassadors for Christ

Did you know that as believers, we are ambassadors of Christ? Paul made this clear when he declared, "We are therefore Christ's ambassadors, as though God were making his appeal *through us*. We implore you *on Christ's behalf*: Be reconciled to God" (2 Corinthians 5:20).

Is it just me, or did the Apostle Paul just inform us that God needs us to plead His case to mankind? How is it possible that the Creator of the universe cannot be effective without me and you? What an awesome honor God has placed on us to serve in some of the highest positions under heaven! This should come as no surprise, since Paul wrote, "Do you not know that we will judge angels?" (1 Corinthians 6:3a). If we understand the magnitude of judging celestial beings once we are in heaven, we should recognize the high calling we have as ambassadors here on earth. Your personal calling in Christ is to be the lead diplomatic official to those you encounter.

Remember that the president relied on the ambassador to do his bidding on foreign soil because he had to live in the homeland. Isn't this God's current situation? In chapter one, I explained that God withdrew Himself from this world the moment man's nature turned to sinfulness and the world became corrupt. This land became foreign to God's nature, as He cannot have fellowship with sin. Essentially, God withdrew Himself to the only truly sovereign soil and appointed us to speak on His behalf on foreign soil. Sure, God draws men by the Holy Spirit prior to our involvement, but our involvement is absolutely pivotal in the success of God's earthly business. Notice that Paul said that God has given us the message of reconciliation as if He were making His appeal through us. He is working through His ambassadors to convey His message to the world.

Just as our relationship with other nations sometimes needs repair, God's relationship with the fallen world needs that same attention. The ambassador is the key to the reconciliation of mankind to God through Christ. We are in this world to be an example to it, but moreover, to implore men to be reconciled to God. Instead of simply living in the foreign land, we need to become active in the reconciliation efforts between Him and His creation.

Aliens and Strangers

We must also recognize that we do not belong in this land anymore, since we are now born of God and have a heavenly home we have not yet seen. We are not citizens of the earth any longer, because our citizenship is now registered in heaven. This land is foreign soil, but we, the ambassadors, are sent by the Commander-in-Chief of the universe to complete His work.

Regarding believers, Peter referred to us as "aliens and strangers in the world" (1 Peter 2:11a). An alien is a person residing on foreign soil and is not a citizen of that land. That is us. "Their mind is on earthly things. But our citizenship is in heaven" (Philippians 3:19b-20a).

We must come to the realization that we are not of this world but are only on temporary assignment to do the Lord's work. America's ambassadors are not citizens of their country of assignment but of the sovereign land from which they were sent. Knowing this, we must not neglect our earthly duties in the strange land where we have been assigned. If America's ambassadors were negligent in their duties, America's national security might be at risk. In the same way, if we are negligent in our duties as God's ambassadors, it could cost unbelievers their eternal security. On a more positive note, if we help to reconcile a person's broken relationship with God, heaven rejoices and a great "Well done!" will be given to the ambassador.

The Modern Myth

A common myth among the modern church says that a believer can simply let his life be the witness without words. That sounds great, and I believed it for a long time but rarely does it work. Anyone who is convinced that "actions speak louder than words" needs to ask themselves one question: How many souls have I won without words? I know this is hard to swallow and goes against the grain of what you may have been taught or believed but please allow me to speak to your heart.

If an ambassador wore a name tag engraved with the title *Ambassador*, lived and worked on the embassy grounds, and was a good American example to the host country, do you think he would be effective in repairing their broken relationship with the United States? Or do you think this lack of action would amount to the critical diplomacy the president had in mind when he nominated him or the Senate's idea of national representation when they voted to confirm him? The Ambassador not only must live a life worthy of a diplomat but also carry out all assigned duties.

Additionally, the diplomatic efforts of the ambassador do not always happen on the grounds of the embassy. The ambassador must get out from behind embassy walls and engage the foreign officials where they are. He or she must enter their lives and build relationships in order to be effective. Similarly, we as ambassadors of Christ cannot lounge at the embassy and expect to fulfill our obligations to the Kingdom of God. We must go out into the foreign land, find the lost, interact with them, and reconcile them to the King of Kings through the Gospel of Jesus Christ. You can do this on a small scale with the people in your daily life, and it doesn't require a lot of words. You would be surprised how powerful your words of encouragement are to a person apart from God. They carry the power of Almighty God.

In summary, God has placed a special calling on your life. He has made you an ambassador to do His work on this earth by entering the dark rooms of this world and leading the occupants to the light switch. This is an awesome honor and shows that God trusts you to speak on His behalf. The Kingdom of God needs you just as much as you need it in order to make the maximum impact on those around you.

This is vital to the mission of God. You are His representative to those closest to you.

So hold your head high, square your shoulders, and carry yourself like an ambassador, because you are called to represent the King of Kings.

4

Called To Be a Witness

"Not called," did you say? Not heard the call, I think you should say. Put your ear down to the Bible and hear God bid you go and pull sinners out of the fire of sin. Put your ear down to the burdened, agonized heart of humanity and listen to its pitiful wail for help.

Go stand by the gates of hell and hear the damned entreat you to go to their father's house and bid their brothers and sisters, and servants and masters not to go there. And then look Christ in the face, whose mercy you have professed to obey, and tell Him whether you will join heart and soul and body and circumstances in the march to publish His mercy to the world.

These are the words of William Booth, the founder of the Salvation Army and a mighty witness for the cause of Christ. He believed it's the church's duty to be witnesses for the Lord to the lost. Many Christians think it isn't their job to witness, but rather God should accomplish this mission alone. They even quote Jesus: "No one can come to me unless the Father who sent me draws him" (John 6:44a).

But a contextual disconnect has occurred in the understanding of this passage. Jesus was not alleviating the evangelistic burden of the world with these words. He simply meant it took the revelation and confirmation of God to believe that He truly was who He claimed to be.

Jesus Taken Out of Context

This event occurred after Jesus fed the five thousand and walked on the Sea of Galilee. The same crowd that followed Him found Him again at Capernaum and began to question Him. "'What must we do to do the work God requires?'" (John 6:28). Jesus responded, "'The work of God is this: to believe in the one he has sent'" (v. 29). He made salvation a matter of faith in the Son of God, which was a catalyst for Him to declare that He was the "bread that came down from heaven" (v. 41). This made the people grumble saying, "'Is this not Jesus, the son of Joseph, whose father and mother we know?'" (v. 42). They were struggling with the fact that someone they knew could be the Son of God.

Jesus then told them that God Himself confirmed that He was the Christ by saying, "No one can come to me unless the Father who sent me draws him" (John 6:44a). The context of this passage was one of revelation and confirmation, not evangelism.

A similar situation occurred when Jesus went to His hometown and began to preach in the synagogue. The people were amazed at His teaching, wisdom, and ability to perform miracles but were offended and said, "Isn't this the carpenter?

Isn't this Mary's son and the brother of James, Joseph, Judas, and Simon? Aren't his sisters here with us?" (Mark 6:3). Again, the crowd was appalled that someone they knew from birth could be more than a mere man.

Jesus responded to their lack of faith in Him by stating, "Only in his hometown, among his relatives and in his own house is a prophet without honor" (Mark 6:4). This passage of Scripture directly corresponds to His encounter in Capernaum above as the people were locals from the same area around Galilee and previously knew Jesus, His parents, and family.

Through these two situations, Jesus was dealing with those who knew Him prior to His ministry yet failed to believe in Him due to their previous knowledge of Him. The statements Jesus made were not sweeping statements regarding evangelism or the Gospel. They merely showed the problems He encountered with those who knew Him prior. It is true that God is the revealer of truth to man through His Holy Spirit, whom John referred to as "the Spirit of truth" (John 16:12).

When properly examined, these passages would be relevant and applicable to an evangelistic encounter only if the unbeliever specifically questioned the lordship of Christ. In any case, these passages certainly do not conflict with other passages regarding evangelism or the Great Commission.

Jesus on Evangelism

If Jesus believed it was God's work to draw men, in the sense that being a witness was not necessary, then He would not have intervened in the following situation the way He did:

Jesus saw a great many people who needed to hear the Gospel throughout the towns and villages He entered. He told His disciples, "The harvest is plentiful but the workers are few. Ask the Lord of the harvest, therefore, to send out workers into his harvest field" (Matthew 9:37-38). The need was for workers to minister to those "without a shepherd" (Matthew 9:36). Jesus immediately sent out the twelve disciples and gave them authority and the following instructions:

As you go, preach this message: "The kingdom of heaven is near." Heal the sick, raise the dead, cleanse those who have leprosy, drive out demons. Freely you have received, freely give. Do not take along any gold or silver or copper in your belts; take no bag for the journey, or extra tunic, or sandals or a staff: for the worker is worth his keep (Matthew 10:7-10).

The Scripture passage above was Jesus' command to those He sent prior to His crucifixion, but He gave another command, the Great Commission, after His resurrection. This command is recorded at the end of Matthew's gospel:

All authority in heaven and on earth has been given to me. Therefore go and make disciples of all nations, baptizing them in the name of the Father and of the Son and

41

of the Holy Spirit, and teaching them to obey everything I have commanded you (Matthew 28:18-19).

Jesus told His people to be the messengers of God to the world. It represents His desire for us to speak on His behalf because He was going to be with the Father in the sovereign land of God. Jesus was clear that we are to reconcile the world back to God by producing followers of Christ. He never gave us a commission simply to go and live a life worthy of a Christian but to go and be a witness and a testimony. We are not called to be passive but to share our faith in a proactive manner.

Our Words Are Vital

It is God's work alone to confirm truth to unbelievers, but it is the job of His people to bring the message. Paul solidified this position when he wrote these words to the Romans:

How, then, can they call on the one they have not believed in? And how can they believe in the one of whom they have not heard? And how can they hear without someone preaching to them? And how can they preach unless they are sent? (Romans 10:14-15)

Paul's rhetorical questions were simply that—rhetorical. The obvious answer to each one of his questions is, "They can't." Unless someone who knows the Gospel is sent to share the Gospel with them, they can't believe because they will not have heard it. He also reiterated the necessity of being a witness when he said, "Consequently, faith comes from hearing the message, and the message is heard through the word of Christ" (Romans 10:17).

A Witness and a Help

This situation can become even more complex when someone has the Gospel but needs a believer to make it real to them through their spoken testimony. In the story of Philip and the Ethiopian eunuch, Philip encountered someone who had the Gospel but still needed to have the Gospel explained to him.

Upon the prompting of an angel of the Lord, Philip set out on a road that leads from Jerusalem to Gaza. On his way, he encountered a eunuch, a servant of the Queen of Ethiopia. The Holy Spirit prompted Philip to stay near the eunuch's chariot, and he heard the man reading Isaiah the prophet.

Philip asked, "'Do you understand what you are reading?'" (Acts 8:30b)

The eunuch responded, "'How can I . . . unless someone explains it to me?'" (v. 31). So he invited Philip to come up and sit with him.

Philip told him the good news of Jesus Christ, and the eunuch was saved and quickly desired to be baptized. Do you see how fast God can work when we deliver His message? Some people are ready to receive Christ but are waiting for God's messenger to show up. This passage supports Paul's position that unbelievers need our message to hear and believe. But the real issue is that the Gospel will profit a man nothing unless he combines it with faith. And, as Paul said, faith comes from hearing the message.

The eunuch had a desire to seek truth, but even he needed Philip the Evangelist to preach into his life before he could believe and be saved. The eunuch had been reading the scriptures but did not have understanding, so he remained in the dark without truth. He might have remained there if Philip had not been obedient to the Lord's call to be a witness.

Numerous additional passages show God's intention for us to reach the lost with His message. For example, the book of James records that "whoever turns a sinner from the error of his way will save him from death and cover over a multitude of sins" (5:20).

Additionally, Solomon, in all his wisdom, recognized the call of God to witness to unbelievers when he wrote, "The fruit of the righteous is a tree of life, and he who wins souls is wise" (Proverbs 11:30). Jude penned, "Be merciful to those who doubt; snatch others from the fire and save them; to others show mercy, mixed with fear—hating even the clothing stained by corrupted flesh" (Jude 22-23).

There are many lost and dying, and we must be a witness to them while there is still time. I hope you can plainly see that some have taken Jesus' words out of context and used them to justify their lack of witnessing. It is true that God works in the unbeliever to confirm what we speak, but unless we speak, there is nothing to confirm. Your words are powerful and are life and hope to those who hear them. When you witness to unbelievers, God is working and speaking through you because He trusts you. Embrace your calling to be a witness and help others find the light switch!

5

The Purpose of Pentecost

Many modern Christians do not understand the purpose of Pentecost or how it relates to evangelism, but what we are about to discover is that Pentecost was designed by God primarily to empower us to witness. When the Spirit of God filled the church on the day of Pentecost in Acts chapter two, the church as we know it was born.

It wasn't born simply to be the church, but for a mission to reconcile the world back to God. The Great Commission provides evidence that Jesus desired His people to evangelize. Through the coming of the Holy Spirit, He empowered His people to accomplish their commission. Prior to His ascension, Jesus left the church with these words:

But you will receive power when the Holy Spirit comes on you, and you will be my witnesses in Jerusalem, and in all Judea and Samaria, and to the ends of the earth (Acts 1:8).

Jesus related that the primary purpose of the church receiving the Holy Spirit was so they could be empowered as witnesses for the purpose of evangelism. A few days after Jesus instructed the disciples to wait for the gift, the Holy Spirit filled the church on the day of Pentecost. When the church was filled with the Holy Spirit, they immediately declared the "wonders of God" (Acts 2:11) in tongues. This fulfilled Christ's words that they (His disciples) would be His witnesses and would begin their evangelistic ministry in Jerusalem. The Holy Spirit's manifestation of tongues was a mighty proclamation to the world that God was calling all men unto Him. Those that heard the tongues related they heard the disciples "declaring the wonders of God in our own tongues" (Acts 2:11).

The newly empowered Peter immediately preached the first Spirit-filled sermon and implored the crowd to "repent and be baptized" (Acts 2:38). An important note in Peter's sermon was his apologetic pleading with the crowd as he warned them to save themselves from this corrupt generation (Acts 2:40). Peter was filled with the Holy Spirit, not simply to repeat the Gospel that he had heard, but to plead with men by the Holy Spirit to escape the wrath to come. This corresponds to Jesus' instructions when He first sent out the twelve disciples to go and preach "the kingdom of heaven is near" (Matthew 10:7).

The entire book of Acts and most of the epistles (letters) are comprised of the mighty exploits of those like Peter, Paul, Barnabas, Apollos, Timothy, and many more who were empowered by the Holy Spirit and responded according to the will of God. Do you see that the immediate response of those who were filled with the Spirit was to radically evangelize wherever they went? Our response to being filled with God's Spirit should be to tell everyone we can about Jesus. We have been given the same Spirit as those in the early church.

My personal experience mirrored that of the early church when I received the Holy Spirit. I immediately began witnessing to my family, co-workers, and even criminals I arrested. I was uncontainable in my preaching about what I had experienced in God. I did not think twice about sharing my faith but boldly proclaimed salvation to anyone who would listen.

God did many mighty works through me during this time as killers, rapists, and drug dealers received the Gospel in my office. Many of these men and women left my office in tears and admitted they would never have received the Gospel under any other circumstances. They thanked me, hugged me, and praised God as they were escorted off to jail to await their trial.

I was so dedicated to the mission to evangelize that I took the Gospel all over the world. On my time off during my government trips, I served as an evangelist to the nations. I shared the Gospel in Muslim countries, in the Orient, in war-torn regions, and even in areas that still had communist sentiments. Nothing had the power to stop me, and nothing can stop you if you embrace your calling to be one of His witnesses.

Societal Pressures Are No Excuse

The environment of our modern world is certainly not friendly to the Gospel of Jesus Christ. Many Christians are hindered in their outspokenness about their faith because of the secularization of most of society and the rejection of biblical teaching. Christians fear mild persecution and experience anxiety when it comes to sharing their faith because of the godless environment they live in. Many people think God doesn't expect them to fulfill the Great Commission in this type of environment, and they're content with simply living quiet Christian lives.

But God made no provision for this in scripture. In fact, the social, religious, and political environment of the early church makes our modern environment seem like a Christian utopia. And even in that time, this was God's command through Paul:

> *Whatever happens, conduct yourselves in a manner worthy of the gospel of Christ. Then, whether I come and see you or only hear about you in my absence, I will know that you stand firm in one spirit, contending as one man for the faith of the gospel without being frightened in any way by those who oppose you.*

> *This is a sign to them that they will be destroyed, but that you will be saved—and that by God. For it has been granted to you on behalf of Christ not only to believe on him, but also to suffer for him, since you are going through the same struggle you saw I had, and now hear that I still have* (Philippians 1:27-30).

It seems there is little willingness to suffer for Christ in our modern time. The pressures of the surrounding society of the early church were greater by far than those in America today. Yet early followers of Jesus Christ evangelized everywhere they went. Why do Christians not share their faith in modern times?

The purpose of this section is not to investigate the effects of societal pressures as factors that suppress evangelism, but to demonstrate that the overwhelming pressure placed on the church of the first century was not enough to silence them from preaching the Gospel. Let's take a look at some of the experiences of our biblical predecessors. Then you can determine whether our modern-day fears are legitimate reasons for failing to fulfill the Great Commission.

On that day [after the stoning of Stephen], *a great persecution broke out against the church in Jerusalem, and all except the apostles were scattered throughout Judea and Samaria. Godly men buried Stephen and mourned deeply for him. But Saul began to destroy the church. Going from house to house, he dragged off men and women and put them in prison. Those who had been scattered preached the Word wherever they went* (Acts 8:1-4).

Fearless and Effective Through Persecution

The book of Acts provides a powerful biblical model for fulfilling the Great Commission, regardless of the circumstances. One day, while Peter and John were preaching to the people about the resurrection, the Sadducees seized them and had them put in jail. When they were brought before the High Priest, Peter spoke boldly by the Holy Spirit, defending the Gospel.

When they saw the courage of Peter and John and realized that they were unschooled, ordinary men, they were astonished and they took note that these men had been with Jesus (Acts 4:13).

First, Peter was fearless in the face of opposition and boldly used the empowerment provided by the Holy Spirit to respond to his accusers. Remember, this is the same Peter who cowardly denied Christ three times prior to his crucifixion. In his book *In Step with the God of all Nations: Discovering the Heartbeat of God*, Philip Steyne describes the reason for this boldness. "The energizing, life-giving Holy Spirit enabled the church to communicate the Gospel and participate in God's mission in the face of all challenges."

Moreover, the scripture clearly indicates that these men were noticeably uneducated but articulated the Gospel with authority. This should encourage believers who feel inadequate to share the Gospel with unbelievers. The Holy Spirit works powerfully through any Christian to deliver the message, so long as the believer is willing.

Last, it was obvious to the accusers that these men had been in the presence of Jesus Christ simply by their powerful testimony and fearlessness in the face of their circumstances. This issue is significant to modern Christians in that boldness in evangelism is a direct result of having been with the Lord.

The disciples had been with Him in person, but we can have fellowship with Him in the Spirit. Through knowing Christ in the salvation relationship and walking with Him daily, we should have the same bold empowerment as those who walked with Christ during His earthly ministry. Perhaps modern Christians are not connected to the Lord frequently enough or possibly are not walking in the fullness of the Spirit of God.

The leaders who cross-examined Peter and John pondered among themselves, trying to decide what to do with them. They could not deny the great miracles the apostles had done, but in order to stop the message of Christ from spreading, they ordered them "not to speak or teach at all in the name of Jesus" (Acts 4:18). Peter and James responded mightily by saying, "Judge for yourselves whether it is right in God's sight to obey you rather than God. For we cannot help speaking about what we have seen and heard" (Acts 4:19-20).

Upon hearing this, they released the men. Peter and John returned to their people and prayed for boldness to speak in light of the Jews' threats. Immediately, the place they were in was shaken and "they were all filled with the Holy Spirit and spoke the word of God boldly" (Acts 4:31).

Do you see that the Holy Spirit provided the boldness to witness without fear? Their lives were at risk, yet they gladly shared the Gospel wherever they went. Most of the apostles were eventually killed because of their radical faith and refusal to keep quiet about it. We too are filled with the Spirit to endure persecution, even to the point of death, and are expected to preach the Gospel anyway. Our modern fear of persecution is no match for the struggles the early church faced, yet they stood boldly in the face of their opposition and preached with the passion of God. We must shake off these excuses and get back to the business of winning souls. Only then will we truly operate in the fullness of the power that came at Pentecost.

A study of the habits of Spirit-filled pioneers of the early 1900s reveals a lifestyle of evangelism. Their newfound experience with Holy Spirit empowerment and the phenomenon of tongues set the precedent for Spirit-empowered living. Their entire lives were connected to the baptism in the Holy Spirit and the results of Spirit-filled living, which was primarily personal evangelism. In his powerful doctoral dissertation, Scott Bottoms reported that the move of God that sparked the great Pentecostal movements of the last century was strikingly similar to the Acts experience of personal and collective evangelism.

The Holy Spirit was the center of life itself, which led them to spread the Gospel as a lifestyle. In his 2007 article in Enrichment Journal, Don Detrick asserts that the "old-time Pentecostals spoke of *having a burden* for the lost. Weeping and crying at the altar because of lost people should be something we experience, not something we read about in church history books." These facts, coupled with the early church's experience, provide a firm foundation for an argument that a primary purpose of every believer's personal empowerment is personal evangelism.

6

The Great Omission

Imagine for a moment ten thousand people lost in a massive cave of total darkness, and one thousand of them had flashlights. There would be plenty of light to go around and enough guides to lead the masses out of the cave. But what if all the flashlights died except ten? Would that not change the dynamic? The ten lights would be vital to the panicking crowd following them. The people with flashlights would have significantly greater impact, and each light would seem a thousand times brighter than before. These few lights would seem as bright as the stars.

We live in a dark and dying world. As it becomes darker and darker, our lights should shine brighter and brighter. Paul told the church in Philippi that they should strive to be "children of God without fault in a crooked and depraved generation" (Philippians 2:15a). He finished his thought by saying: "Then you will shine among them like stars." Paul was saying that if we stay closely connected to God, our power source, and keep ourselves untainted by the world, we will have even greater opportunity to shine because of the absence of light around us. As we grow closer in relationship to God and conform to the image of His Son, we will shine even brighter in this wicked and crooked generation and become beacons of hope among those in darkness.

So why are we failing to reach our world? As Christians, we are called and commissioned to the task of winning souls. But for many in the church world today, the Great Commission has become the Great Omission. Luis Palau, in his 1997 article titled "The Church's Forgotten No. 1 Priority" in *Enrichment Journal*, describes this dilemma as follows: "We know His final command to 'go and make disciples of all nations' (Matthew 28:19) as the Great Commission, not the great suggestion." In Scott Bottoms' dissertation on evangelism, he related that only when churches "recapture the Great Commission as the defining purpose of their existence will our nation be effectively reached." Does God's mission of evangelizing the world define our purpose? Are we out of touch with our Christian reality? Have we lost our calling? The following research will shed ample light on these issues.

In 2005, the Barna Group conducted a study called "How Christians Share Their Faith." At first glance, it seems to paint a rosy picture of Christians' witnessing habits. The study found that "two-thirds of evangelicals (66%) had shared their faith, compared to just two-fifths (41%) of those who are associated with mainline churches."

These statistics suggest that the work of the commission is being accomplished in part, but a deeper look at Barna's study is more revealing. Christians frequently used several methods to evangelize, the study revealed, but "the most prolific method was to 'offer to pray with a non-Christian who was in need of encouragement or support.'" Almost eight out of ten Christians (78 percent) surveyed said they had used this method in the past year.

This type of witnessing has its place, but it seems a bit passive, reactive, and infrequent. While a great majority of Christians surveyed claimed they had prayed with an unbeliever, they had done so only once in the last year, according to Barna. The mere fact that Barna reported this approach to evangelism as the most widely used indicates that Christians are not embracing biblical evangelism, but rather a more passive, inconspicuous, and infrequent form of spiritual encouragement. The biblical model of evangelism is to go and "tell the people the full message of this new life" (Acts 5:20b). From Barna's report, it seems that people have replaced God's version of witnessing with a more palatable and passive one.

Knowing what you already know of the Apostle Paul, could you imagine him simply offering to pray with someone in a crisis and not sharing the full message of the Gospel with him? I can't either. I believe he would have already shared the Gospel to equip the person before the crisis came. More importantly, I believe his words would always be seasoned with true love—not worldly love, but love that communicates itself in a desperate plea for the soul and not just the present crisis.

I liken this to the story in chapter one. Many modern Christians are like the people who had light in their rooms and left their doors cracked open in case those in darkness happened to stumble upon it. A more sufficient fulfillment of the Great Commission is the man who took his light throughout the house and helped others to find a light of their own. It was an active pursuit, not a passive one. It was relentless, not relative.

Instead of waiting for a crisis, Christians should proactively witness to their friends. We should tell them of the mighty power of God so they might avoid the crisis, or at least know Him and call out to Him if they do encounter trouble. Paul the Apostle wrote, "Now is the time of God's favor, now is the day of salvation" (2 Cor. 6:2b). We, as Christians, should implore those around us toward faith in Christ before it is too late. Christians are called to a passionate and bold lifestyle of fulfilling the Great Commission. While the passive methods are noble and compassionate, they are far from the full measure of the Great Commission. This hardly fulfills the command of our Lord or even comes close to anything we see in the Bible.

In 2012, Lifeway Research conducted a study that reveals much more about the evangelism habits of Christians. John Wilke summarized this study in a Lifeway Research article called *Churchgoers Believe in Sharing Their Faith, Most Never Do*. The name alone reveals the problem. As I mentioned earlier, Lifeway Research found that 80 percent of Christians surveyed believed they have a personal responsibility to share their faith with non-Christians. Yet only "25 percent say they have shared their faith once or twice, and 14 percent have shared three or more times over the last six months." These numbers are astonishingly low and indicate a problem. But according to the study, the problem cannot be societal pressures. In fact, 75 percent of those surveyed related they "feel comfortable" that they can share the Gospel with an unbeliever effectively. Additionally, 83 percent disagreed with the following statement: "I am hesitant to let others know that I am a Christian."

According to Lifeway's research, believers know and accept that they are called to evangelize and feel confident in their abilities to do so. Yet only a quarter of them had even embraced this admitted calling in the past six months. What is the disconnect between the knowledge of God's calling and the fulfillment of it? How is it possible that we can so blatantly disregard the task we have been given—especially when there are lost and dying people all around us? Do we even consider the expectations of God in our daily lives? Do we have any compassion for those who are on a one-way road to hell?

I thought it was interesting that Lifeway's initial study was an attempt to measure spiritual maturity in believers. They narrowed their scope to eight issues that are essential for the maturing of a believer. Of the eight, "Sharing Christ" had the lowest average among Protestant church attendees. I can't think of seven other factors that outweigh or overshadow the commission to share Jesus with others. I can think of only one: growing closer to the heart of God in my own life. Out of this relationship with God should flow a desire for relationships with others that will bring opportunities to share the Gospel of Jesus Christ.

Why the Omission of the Commission?

In William Abraham's book *The Logic of Evangelism*, he writes that evangelism has "been relegated to a position of minor importance" and "overall has failed to fire the imaginations of the leaders of the central ecclesiastical institutions." While I believe this is true, the problem is not so complex. I believe there are many contributing factors that can explain much of the church's failure to evangelize, but all of these factors are the result of a deeper, simpler issue: the lack of revivalism.

Gaines Dobbins saw this issue creeping in as early as 1948. In his *Review and Expositor* article, he said the "wane of revivalism means the wane of evangelism." As the church grows further from the heart of God, it will grow further from the Spirit-led mission of God. No amount of evangelism training alone will solve the problem. Only revival in the church will spark the mission again.

We can turn this world around only when Christians return to the heart of God. The job of evangelism is one of the Spirit, so if Christians have lost their fervor for the Lord, they will no longer hear the call to seek the lost. Moreover, if Christian leaders have lost their calling and have failed to equip the church, the effects will be even more devastating. I believe we have a combination of both.

As I stated in the previous chapter, Scott Bottoms believes that the Holy Spirit empowerment of the believer has been misinterpreted in modern times. In his dissertation, he related that the history of the last one hundred years of

Spirit-led churches shows a shift from one of "personal empowerment for witness to an emphasis on personal enrichment and church vitality." In the early 1900s, Spirit-filled believers saw their empowerment as an equipping to win the lost. I believe Bottoms is correct that some modern-day churches see the Spirit-filling as value only to their personal gifts and their church's spiritual prosperity.

Bottoms also related that the focus of the church has taken more of a humanitarian approach to world issues, as opposed to that of Spirit-led evangelism. Have you not seen the shift yourself? Most churches that I know are dedicated to impacting their community through one humanitarian cause or another but have not made a concerted effort to pull sinners from the fire and save them. No number of car washes, parades, or service projects can replace authentic sharing of the Gospel. All these social justice and humanitarian projects fall short of the Great Commission.

Another major problem hindering the church's impact is not the lack of training but a lack of training based on true biblical models of evangelism. Scott Bottoms refers to this problem as "the decreasing priority of an effective communication of the Gospel." Churches are teaching five-step programs to help their members share the Gospel but have not considered the New Testament examples in their teaching. The book of Acts and the epistles (letters) record countless evangelism encounters involving Peter, Paul, James, Apollos, and others, which serve as the supreme models of New Testament evangelism. This is what we should be teaching and practicing. I'm an advocate for creative methods, so I will show, mainly through Paul's model of evangelism, that we should use creativity when encountering an unbeliever.

In summary, Christianity suffers as a result of the lack of personal testimony. Many Christians do not embrace their proactive role in fulfilling the Great Commission personally. Instead, they are reactive at best, not actively seeking to share the Gospel. "Christian missions" has taken the form of local church support to foreign missions, but we don't see much evidence of missions in the daily life of the individual believer. This dilemma is reconcilable. When Christians are trained and equipped in their responsibility to witness, things can begin to change. This training can take many forms, but when Christians are trained in biblical models of evangelism, we can reach souls effectively.

This issue is not one of training alone, but also of innate, born-again purpose. This issue may stem from a lack of true spiritual power in the lives of modern Christians because, as Ben Witherington reported in his commentary, "without the coming of the Spirit there would be no prophecy, no preaching, no mission, no conversions, and no worldwide Christian movement." Let's turn this omission back into a commission by committing ourselves to leading others out of the dark rooms of this world and to the light switch.

7

The Watchman

The *Titanic*'s maiden voyage began on April 10, 1912 from her dock in Southampton, England. Her destination was New York, and the world awaited word of her majestic arrival. As the *Titanic* left the dock, the wake of the great vessel was so massive that it caused a nearby ship (SS *New York*) to break away from her moorings and drift dangerously close to the *Titanic*. This incident almost ended her journey before she started, which probably would have been a better fate for all on board. Some may have been humbled for a moment and considered disembarking the vessel at one of their two stops, but none did. After visiting a couple of docks in northern Europe, the *Titanic* sailed for America.

The ship carried 2,223 souls from all walks of life. The finest things for the finest people were offered on the *Titanic*. Some paid almost one hundred thousand dollars in modern exchange for a maiden voyage ticket on the majestic steamship. This was considered a chance of a lifetime. The passengers' faith in the ship was secure, and their minds were on much more important matters, like her luxurious dining rooms, fairytale-like ballrooms, and five-star sleeping quarters. She was commanded by a more-than-capable captain. The crew and staff were fit for a king. The world had poured their best efforts and resources into this beautiful work of oceanic engineering and hospitality. The passengers placed their fate firmly into the hull of the mighty vessel and the world's testimony of her unsinkable qualities. After all, this was the greatest work of man ever to sail the high seas.

Five days and four frigid nights passed, and the *Titanic* and its precious cargo were close to finishing their historic journey. The Captain, Edward Smith, had received wireless radio transmissions warning of icebergs in the path of his ship in the days prior, which caused him to alter the ship's course slightly.

The ship was equipped with two Marconi radios powered by 1,500 watts of electricity and employed two radio operators, Jack Phillips and Harold Bride. They worked in shifts to ensure constant communication between the ship and land. The men also sent and received messages for the passengers, which was a lucrative venture for the Marconi Company. Beginning in the early afternoon of April 14, the Marconi operators began receiving messages from the steamer *Amerika* and more from the *Mesaba*, stating that icebergs were spotted in the path of the *Titanic*.

The Marconi operators were so busy with the profitable passenger messages that they ignored the warnings and never relayed them to the captain. The operators may have seen icebergs before and assumed they were no match for their unsinkable fortress. The fate of 2,223 people hung in the balance, but the men they depended on for their safety were distracted by the moment and their daily earnings. Then evening began to wind down and many of the passengers probably departed the evening shows, retired to their cabins, and drifted off to sleep.

The crow's nest towered over the deck and smokestacks, providing a breathtaking view of the north Atlantic. The air was frigid but the water was calm. The two lookouts on duty that night were Fredrick Fleet and Reginald Lee.

At about twenty minutes before midnight, the infamous moment came with a crow's nest alarm that rang out in fury, "Iceberg, right ahead!" Immediately the captain and crew did everything possible to steer clear of their doom, but it was too late for the maiden vessel, and she struck its massive wall beneath the waterline.

At first, the passengers were alarmed, but they still staked their faith in their ship's unsinkable reputation. The same radio operators who refused to pass the seemingly useless messages were now sending distress signals out by the droves. Several ships received the signals, but none were close enough to reach the *Titanic* in time. Nothing could save her as her lower compartments quickly filled with water.

The ship's protocol called for the lifeboats to be lowered and filled with people. However, the initial lifeboats were sent out with only a fraction of the seats filled, not only because of the "women and children first" rule, but also because people still weren't convinced that they needed to be rescued.

As the next two hours rushed by in what seemed like a few minutes, everyone on board scurried to and scuffled over the remaining seats on the lifeboats. Many never got a seat and were forced either to jump into the freezing waters or wait it out with the broken vessel. This was due, in part, to a shortage of lifeboats to support the large passenger load. Shortly after two o'clock a.m. on April 15, the unsinkable ship sank to her new resting place on the sea floor, never to sail again. Of the 2,223 passengers, only 706 survived.

Isn't it a shame how many people had to die on the *Titanic* because of the failures of just a few? Imagine if the negligent ones had listened to the warnings and had alerted others. And imagine if the people would have seen the danger of trying to stay aboard the ship after it struck the iceberg. Every lifeboat would have been filled, and there would have been many more survivors than 706, although there were certainly not enough lifeboats to save everyone.

While reading this story of disaster that could have been avoided, what do you think of the failures of the captain, crew, and radio operators? Would you have done differently? Would you have warned the passengers that icebergs were reported in the path of the *Titanic*? Would you have convinced them they were in need of a lifeboat? Or would you have been content with your reserved seat and kept quiet? Remember your answers to these questions as you continue to read.

The *Titanic*-Sized Problem

At the beginning of time, a ship called Mankind broke away from her moorings and set off on a maiden voyage that was never meant to be. God had a perfect plan for us, but we chose not to stay docked, and because of sin, our fellow*ship* had been broken with our Lord. Never again could our ship return to her docks because sin destroyed them.

Our relationship with God could never be as it once was, but this was not the end of His plan. The Lord had to allow us to take a journey on the sea of choices. The finest things were offered on the ship of Mankind as she enticed the hearts of men and women away from the Lord with her grandeur and the pleasures of this life. Over time, God has attempted to steer the hearts of its passengers back toward Him, but the world's allure has prevailed.

As the journey toward the Day of the Lord continues, the passengers have grown more comfortable with the world and are willing to pay a great price to stay on board. The passenger list is innumerable and is comprised of people from all nations. The people have staked their faith in the world's comforts and enduring reputation. Many priests and prophets have attempted to persuade the leaders that the ship's course is deadly, but the leaders continued to convince the people that the world was still unsinkable, and they altered their course only slightly.

Along the way, those who have come to Christ have made a reservation for a seat on the lifeboat of salvation. They were also given a message to warn people of coming tribulation.

Initially, the followers of Christ passionately pursued those who walked the ship's deck in darkness, but as the church age has progressed, they have begun ignoring them and have become more concerned about the people's affairs and their own. The lost passengers have become more enthralled in the entertainment and pampering the world offers. They rarely consider the judgment of God. Sadly, many of the messengers of God have fallen into this same slumber and lost their calling. At this point, life's passengers consider an iceberg of tribulation to be no match for this great world and have grown in their confidence that it is still unsinkable.

We are now in the final night of life's cruise, and most of the passengers have retired to their quarters and drifted off to sleep without a worry in the world or a thought about their God. The air is cold, the night waters are calm, but trouble is on its way. One last warning is being sent, and it reads, "Iceberg straight ahead; this ship's goin' down."

Sadly, this world is on a course of destruction, and God has placed the object of tribulation directly in its path. No amount of maneuvering will avoid the collision; only a seat on the lifeboat will provide escape from what is to come. In just a few years, the world will be engulfed in wrath, and the unsinkable will sink in a great fury of judgment. But there is a lifeboat whose hull is built on the crossbeams of Christ Himself, which are more than adequate to support this world's passenger load. Only He can save the passengers, but someone must convince them that they need rescued.

Isn't this the current state of our world? We are all passengers on a ship that's going down. This world is headed for the greatest iceberg in history, but most don't even realize it. Those who do are so focused on completing the work of this world that they don't have time to warn people. There is no way this ship is ever going to reach land again.

God has called you and me to serve as night watchmen in the crow's nest of life. He has shown us the great unavoidable iceberg of tribulation that's going to sink this world and all who are still passengers within it. Just because we have a seat reserved on a lifeboat doesn't mean it is time to relax and wait to be hoisted down. We must urgently inform the passengers to get on the only lifeboat that can save them: Jesus Christ.

Most of the passengers see an iceberg for only what is visible above the waterline. From this perspective, most icebergs don't seem that intimidating. But most of the time, only a small fraction of the iceberg is above water. When a rather small piece of ice sticks out of the water, a massive wall of devastation can lurk beneath. This world focuses on what is seen, but we focus on the eternal. We as believers know what lurks beneath the waterline, and it is our duty and obligation to get the word out. Please read and try to digest this passage from Ezekiel 33:1-9.

> *The word of the Lord came to me: "Son of man, speak to your countrymen and say to them: 'When I bring the sword against a land, and the people of the land choose one of their men and make him their watchman, and he sees the sword coming against the land and blows the trumpet to warn the people, then if anyone hears the trumpet but*

does not take warning and the sword comes and takes his life, his blood will be on his own head. Since he heard the sound of the trumpet but did not take warning, his blood will be on his own head. If he had taken warning, he would have saved himself. But if the watchman sees the sword coming and does not blow the trumpet to warn the people and the sword comes and takes the life of one of them, that man will be taken away because of his sin, but I will hold the watchman accountable for his blood.'

"Son of man, I have made you a watchman for the house of Israel; so hear the word I speak and give them warning from me. When I say to the wicked, 'O wicked man, you will surely die,' and you do not speak out to dissuade him from his ways, that wicked man will die for his sin, and I will hold you accountable for his blood. But if you do warn the wicked man to turn from his ways and he does not do so, he will die for his sin, but you will have saved yourself."

The Lord gave Ezekiel a dire warning that if he failed to do his job and warn the people, he would be held accountable for what happened to them. But if he carried out his mission to warn them, he would not be held accountable, whatever their response. God called Ezekiel to be a watchman for the people because He cared for them, and He expected the watchman to fulfill his commission.

For a while, I believed this scripture was speaking only to Ezekiel's specific situation to warn the Old Testament Jews, but then I read the Apostle Paul's use of the same watchman principle in the New Testament. Paul was in Corinth, where he continually reasoned with Jews and Greeks about the lordship of Christ. Consider his words to them:

But when the Jews opposed Paul and became abusive, he shook out his clothes in protest and said to them, *"Your blood be on your own heads! I am clear of my responsibility.* From now on I will go to the Gentiles" (Acts 18:6).

Paul was operating as a watchman under the same warning from the Lord that Ezekiel was given. He knew he had a mandate to warn the lost of the coming wrath of God. He also knew that if he failed to warn the people, God would judge him. This shows that God will not bring His wrath upon a person who has not been warned, but He will hold the watchman accountable for failing to obey his commission.

You and I have been made watchmen to the lost people in our daily lives. The watchmen on the *Titanic* shouted their warning when they saw the iceberg, realizing the devastation that lurked beneath the waterline, but they were too late. The radio operators, who had been informed of the iceberg long before anyone saw it, had failed to warn the people.

Ezekiel saw the wrath of God coming against his people, Israel, and warned them to save themselves. Paul understood his position as a watchman and attempted to warn the Corinthian Jews of their lost condition without Christ. Both men recognized their personal responsibility to warn the people.

Why would we be any different? Throughout scripture, God has warned us that the Great Tribulation of God's wrath is coming upon the people of this fallen world. We have been warned of the horrors of hell and the need for mankind to turn from their wicked ways or face its fury. Do you remember how you felt after reading that the *Titanic* disaster could have been avoided? Do you remember making judgments about those who failed to warn the people, failed to steer the ship clear of disaster, failed to convince the people to get in the lifeboats? If we, knowing the disaster that is coming upon this world, have not warned those around us, we are no different than those in charge of the *Titanic*.

We need to realize that we operate under a commission to win souls but ultimately to warn the people of the coming wrath of God. Remember that when Jesus first sent His disciples out to evangelize, He instructed them to warn people that the Kingdom of heaven was near.

Jude spoke of the same urgency when he related that we should "be merciful to those who doubt; snatch others from the fire and save them; to others show mercy, mixed with fear" (Jude 22a). And during Peter's great sermon after the Spirit moved on the Day of Pentecost, he warned the people to save themselves from this corrupt generation (Acts 2:40).

We have been entrusted with the information that can save this generation. We can make a huge impact on the lives of those around us by simply sharing it rather than keeping it to ourselves. Our words are a lifeline that will lead them to the lifeboat of Jesus Christ.

Let's begin to show unbelievers that this world will soon pass away, but they don't have to go down with the ship. If we share this vital information, the world will see our compassion for them, and many will leave their dark cabins, rise to the deck, and follow us to the lifeboat.

You are a watchman. Sound the alarm!

8

A–Paul-o-getics

One day, while I was conducting an open forum at work, a co-worker asked some deep theological questions, and I answered them. An older gentleman stood and stated, "This is not an evangelistic forum, and I would appreciate it if you would stop discussing your religion."

He had been brainwashed, like many people, to believe we should not discuss religion in the workplace and felt he had the right to demand my silence on the issue.

I stood up and passionately defended the Gospel by saying, "John, where were you when I needed you most? Where were you when I was the lone defender of morality in this office and asked everyone to stop discussing sexually explicit matters and using foul language? As outspoken as you are about the inappropriateness of my religious conversation, I'm surprised you didn't see the inappropriateness of those other conversations and make as bold a stand."

John then said, "Point taken," and sat down.

I never again heard any dissent to my openness about Christianity in that office. I defended the Gospel by standing up for it.

This was one of Paul's greatest traits. Everywhere he went, he not only looked for an opportunity to share the Gospel, but he was a defender of it as well. He didn't allow people to push the Gospel out of society, but he kept it alive and well by speaking out about it. If I had obeyed John's superficial demand to stop discussing my faith, I never again would have been able to share it openly because a social norm that was already established in people's minds would have been tested and reinforced.

We've all been told not to discuss politics or religion in public because with so many differing views, there was a good chance of getting into a heated debate. Well, this worldly way of thinking has crept into the church and made Christians cower and keep silent. Not only should we discuss our faith, but we should share it with boldness, fueled by love and not weakness sprinkled with cowardice. Many of us fall prey to false restrictions and biblical misconceptions about sharing our faith.

Some Christians think they shouldn't debate about the validity of the Gospel or passionately persuade their friends to give their lives to the Lord. Since most Christians abide by these unwritten rules, you would think they came from the Bible, right? As a matter of fact, these made-up rules are not biblical. They're the opposite of the examples we see in the Bible.

Paul serves as our greatest model of evangelism, aside from the Lord Himself. Paul's normal mode of evangelism was a commitment to do whatever it took to win the soul. The word "apologetics" is a theological term used to describe the defense of the Gospel. I titled this chapter "A-Paul-o-getics" because he (Paul) is the Bible's greatest apologist (someone who logically, reasonably, and passionately defends the Gospel), and I think it is fitting to remember his example in the very center of the term apologetics.

Evangelism teaching misses the mark when it strays from the models in the Bible. Much of modern teaching has focused on action but not the preaching of the Gospel the way the early church did. We have succumbed to a Christian culture of subtleties, and it has not been effective. Some Christians have used this statement by Saint Francis of Assisi to excuse themselves from evangelizing with words: "Preach the Gospel always; when necessary, use words." I understand that your actions should give your words validity, but they can never replace the spoken word of testimony to an unbeliever. Saint Francis had a good point, but I don't think he was telling us not to evangelize. Instead, we should let the light of our actions shine on a daily basis. I interpret "when necessary" as referring to an evangelism encounter. Either way, the biblical model of evangelism should serve as our guide.

Let's consider some of those encounters in the New Testament that I have been referring to. You'll see Paul's clear apologetic pattern of reasoning with people and persuading them to accept the Gospel.

In Thessalonica, Paul went to the synagogue on three Sabbath days and "reasoned with them from the Scriptures, explaining and proving that the Christ had to suffer and rise from the dead" (Acts 17:2b-3a). Paul's apologetic (defense) approach to spreading the Gospel became his norm wherever the Lord sent him. In fact, he related in his letter to the Philippians: "I am put here for the *defense* of the Gospel" (Philippians 1:16). Paul also declared: "This Jesus I am proclaiming to you is the Christ . . ." (Acts 17:3b). His evangelism methods of reasoning, explaining, and proving resulted in many people in Thessalonica becoming followers of Christ. This included some Jews, a large number of God-fearing Greeks, and many prominent women.

In Corinth, Paul used these same methods, and every Sabbath he reasoned with Jews and Greeks and tried to persuade them that Jesus was the Christ. In fact, Paul stated that these were his exact intentions when he wrote his second letter to the Christians in Corinth: "Since, then, we know what it is to fear the Lord, we try to persuade men" (2 Corinthians 5:11a). Paul made no bones about his apologetic and persuasive methods of sharing the Gospel, and he wrote to others, hoping they would do the same.

In Ephesus, Paul continued reasoning with the Jews, and his apologetic pattern of evangelism laid the groundwork for a man named Apollos to come to Ephesus and boldly speak in the synagogue. The Bible is clear that Apollos "vigorously refuted the Jews in public debate, proving from the Scriptures that Jesus was the Christ" (Acts 18:28). This pattern, which Paul established and Apollos continued, provides ample foundation for the development of a biblical model for effective, Spirit-led evangelism. But in case you're still skeptical, I will provide more details.

Paul in Athens

At this point, it may seem that the common thread in Paul's apologetic encounters was reasoning with the Jews in the synagogue. However, his activities in Athens caused his ministry to take a different direction and support a general method of evangelism, regardless of audience. When Paul was in Athens, he "reasoned in the Synagogue" (Acts 17:17), but the avenue he found for witnessing to the Gentiles was in the marketplace.

Some Stoic and Epicurean philosophers invited Paul to the Aereopogus, also known as Mars Hill, which was a place of public debate and reasoning reserved for the wisest and most learned Gentile men in Athens. At the Areopagus, Paul took advantage of the opportunity he was given to present the Gospel of Jesus Christ, and by the leading of the Holy Spirit, he shared the Gospel in a most unusual and creative way. Paul related to the unbelievers' current situation and surroundings as an avenue to drive the Gospel:

Men of Athens! I see that in every way you are very religious. For as I walked around and looked carefully at your objects of worship, I even found an altar with this inscription: To an Unknown God. Now what you worship as something unknown I am going to proclaim to you (Acts 17:22-23).

His complimentary introduction not only flattered his highly esteemed audience, but it also established common ground of religion between him and the men of Athens. He was essentially saying, "Look, I know you are religious, and so am I. Let's reason together." Paul probably saw this as necessary to ensure solid rapport had been established with his audience prior to introducing the new teaching of Christ. F.F. Bruce examined Paul's approach and wrote, "The preaching of the Gospel to pagans naturally required a different technique from preaching it to Jews and God-fearers" (Bruce 1942, 14). I believe Paul was reasoning with his audience through creative approaches, which would then provide access to the heart. Then the audience would have open ears to receive the Gospel.

Paul knew his audience and specifically tailored his approach to meet their cultural and religious perspectives. To ensure a proper springboard for the Gospel, Paul used what was familiar to the Athenian men—their idols—to capture their attention and lower their defensiveness and skepticism. He preached the Gospel to those present, won a few of them to the Lord, and was asked to return and speak further on the subject. Let's go even deeper into Paul's evangelistic journeys and see how he responded to those in authority.

Paul's Ultimate Apologetic Before Powerful Men

The consummation of Paul's apologetic ministry occurred upon his arrest and appeal to Caesar himself. Satan attempted to use people in authority to shut Paul up, just as he'd tried to use my co-worker John to shut me up. But as you will see through the following examples, Paul didn't let anything extinguish the Gospel—not even jail bars and prison walls. He first appeared before Felix, the governor in Caesarea. He presented his defense, saying he was no more than a peaceful follower of the Way and was now on trial for teaching on "the resurrection of the dead" (Acts 24:21). Felix, who was well acquainted with the Way, waited a few days before making his judgment. He then sent for Paul and asked to hear him speak about his faith in Jesus Christ.

Instead of trying to get himself out of trouble, Paul used this opportunity to preach the Gospel unwaveringly and "discoursed on righteousness, self-control and the judgment to come" (Acts 24:25). Upon hearing this, Felix felt conviction and was afraid because he had been unjust to many and had lusted after another man's wife.

After two more years of imprisonment, Felix was succeeded by Governor Festus, who almost immediately dealt with Paul's situation. Festus offered Paul an opportunity to change jurisdictions and go before his court in Jerusalem, but Paul appealed to Caesar. Festus felt it inadequate to send a Roman citizen to Caesar without any formal charges against him, so he asked King Agrippa to hear Paul's case as a second opinion. Paul was permitted to defend his innocence to Agrippa, but he could not forsake the Gospel, even though his life was on the line. Paul told Agrippa the story of his conversion and took the opportunity to share the Gospel by telling him the words that Jesus had spoken to him: "I am sending you to them to open their eyes and turn them from darkness to light, and from the power of Satan to God" (Acts 26:17b-18a).

Agrippa grew frustrated (and probably convicted) and said, "Your great learning is driving you insane" (Acts 26:24b). Paul responded apologetically and stated, "What I am saying is true and reasonable. The king is familiar with these things, and I can speak freely to him. I am convinced that none of this has escaped his notice, because it was not done in a corner" (Acts 26:25b-26).

Then Paul went for it. He abandoned his own defense and attempted to reach King Agrippa with the Gospel by asking him, "King Agrippa, do you believe the prophets? I know you do" (verse 27). Agrippa, feeling the full weight of this Gospel being preached to him, responded: "Do you think that in such a short time you can persuade me to be a Christian?" (verse 28).

This proves that Paul was making the most of every opportunity to defend the faith and preach the Gospel to everyone he encountered, regardless of his audience or circumstances. Christians can learn a great deal from this and not only look for opportunities to share the Gospel, but also make opportunities when necessary.

Paul's logic and reasoning with Agrippa demonstrated the continuation of a pattern of apologetic ministry. This pattern of reasoning and persuading unbelievers can serve as a model for modern Christians to present the Gospel creatively without changing it. We can do this by allowing the Holy

Spirit to use our knowledge and understanding of our audience to develop rapport as a basis for sharing the Gospel, and then passionately and apologetically sharing it by the leading of the Holy Spirit. Christians should view Paul's ministry as an example but also as permission to change their understanding. Our work is to share the Gospel and to reason with their minds so the Holy Spirit can have access to the heart. Then, and only then, can we turn their hearts from darkness to light.

The world today is much like the world Paul struggled with. Knowledge has increased, false teachings are abundant, and people are spiritually confused. The pattern Paul established is vital to the impact we make on those around us. Logic, reasoning, debate, and passionate persuasion are tools we must see as not only permissible but also necessary to reach those in this generation. We need to stand up for the Gospel and not allow it to be extinguished. We must defend it as Paul did but also reason with unbelievers and prove to them that the Gospel is true.

Most people in this generation are stumbling around in dark rooms and need someone to persuade them that the power source is both faithful and true. Only then will they be persuaded to follow us to the light switch and allow their world to be illuminated.

9

The World of Walls

Pre-Surge Iraq

After the initial invasion and liberation of Iraq from Saddam's regime, the US military enjoyed a short time of celebration and rest from full combat operations. Everyone thought the war was won and our troops could spend the next little while stabilizing the country and then make it home by Christmas (figuratively speaking). Well, it turns out this was a different kind of war that we had merely just begun. The terrorist and insurgent groups that were supported by outside nations began to take advantage of the situation, move in, and infiltrate the Iraqi cities, primarily Baghdad.

These criminals had one agenda: to ensure the failure of the United States. You see, we would have been out of Iraq years earlier if it weren't for the obstructionist countries that poured their entire national efforts into sabotaging our operations and destabilizing Iraq. The terrorists and insurgents worked under the cover of night, blended into the population and, like cowards, frustrated our efforts to bring stability to the fledgling democracy. These groups were becoming increasingly more organized, better funded, and more successful as the days went on. Our highest leadership could not figure out this invisible enemy. US forces began losing hundreds of soldiers to Improvised Explosive Devices (IEDs), rocket attacks, and roadside bombs. Yet we faced no formal enemy and certainly were not winning the war.

These terrorists and insurgents initially crept in from other countries, but they began recruiting locals to join the fight. So external forces were allowed to creep into an open border and corrupt the minds of the Iraqi people, who one day viewed the US forces as liberators and the next day as enemy occupiers.

As the next couple of years passed, the US forces gained little ground in Iraq. They spent most of their time dodging IEDs and rockets while simultaneously attempting to build infrastructure and win the hearts and minds of the Iraqi people. This was not working and America began losing more troops than anyone ever expected. The enemy had gained ground and kept it; we had gained none. Due to the high casualty rate, US forces began withdrawing to safety zones to minimize the number of soldiers getting killed or injured. We began spending more time in camps because that seemed to be the safest place for us, but our preoccupation with safety caused us to make poor strategic decisions.

At that point the enemy began targeting our camps. Normally, under the cover of darkness, the enemy would launch a series of rockets or mortars at a strategic location on the American camp where they anticipated the highest number of casualties. The enemy in Iraq crafted the most ingenious, ever-evolving devices meant to make the maximum impact on the target. Many times the enemy aimed at chow halls, tents, or recreation centers. The key was to aim where they would be guaranteed success.

I was almost a victim of one of these major attacks on a chow hall in Mosul, Iraq, in December 2004. I was working in Baghdad and was scheduled to travel to Mosul the next day, but my boss unexpectedly asked me to stay in Baghdad for another day. God was protecting me because the next day a suicide bomber walked into the chow hall on the camp in Mosul and detonated a bomb vest, killing many soldiers. I probably would have been sitting right there.

Attacks like this caused us to erect a world of walls to protect us from the outside forces that wanted to destroy us. But these walls also kept us from impacting the Iraqi people with a message of hope. The US military spent hundreds of millions of dollars in the construction of this world of walls surrounding every tent, trailer, chow hall, chapel, latrine, and virtually everything else in our camps throughout the country. These walls were our blast barriers to protect us from the incoming fire of the enemy. The world of walls consisted of thousands of fourteen-foot high concrete walls, which we referred to as T-Walls. They were called T-walls because they have a flanged base, and if you flip one upside-down, it looks like the letter "T."

The T-walls were about five feet wide and about eighteen

inches thick. They were notched on the sides, which allowed them to fit together neatly and create a lock-tight blast barrier, protecting the troops. This world of walls was designed in a way so that, no matter where the enemy's attack hit, the walls contained it to a specific area and minimized its impact. Even though there was no overhead cover to keep the impact from occurring, we managed and minimized the impact by compartmentalizing our lives.

The people within a section of trailers might never have known the people living in the section of trailers next to them because they disappeared behind the walls and hardly ever interacted with those around them. This world of walls extended well past the living quarters, though. When I left my living quarters, I went from one world of walls to another and passed people as they faded into other openings in the walls. It was almost weird, how we lived in Iraq. I went from the living quarters to an open area, then to another walled compound that surrounded the chow hall, then to another containing the PX (like a store), then back to my living quarters.

This concept is similar to the methods used to contain forest fires. An area of forest is sectioned off into several smaller portions and divided by firebreaks. These firebreaks ensure that the fire does not spread to the other areas because the trees have all been removed and the dirt has been turned. That leaves a gap between flammable areas to starve the fire out at each edge of that section. This is another ingenious way to contain the effects of a disaster.

For a while, the world of walls minimized the enemy's

impact. But it also minimized our impact. This was the strategic flaw the US forces never could have foreseen. As we retreated to secure locations and failed to stay on the offensive, the enemy flourished. I am not criticizing our tactics whatsoever, just giving a simple overview of the evolution of the Iraq war for illustration purposes.

When we decreased our interaction and presence in the communities of Iraq, the enemy increased theirs. Each time the US forces fought to take a neighborhood and win the hearts of the people, we gained some ground. The problem was that we had to return to our camps for safety, and then the enemy moved back in and reorganized even stronger than before, winning back the hearts of the people through fear. We took one step forward and two steps back until the surge. Our mistake was to retreat to our world of walls while the enemy was allowed free reign of the hearts and minds of the Iraqi people. One thing to note: even though we retreated to our safe zones, the enemy did not stop attacking us. They had us right where they wanted us: defenseless and ineffective.

The Surge

The Department of Defense (DOD) knew they needed to take a drastically different course of action so this war would not turn into the next Vietnam. The American public was desperate for a solution when DOD called on General David Petraeus, who was the Army's premier counterinsurgency expert. Only when General Petraeus called for the surge did the US begin to take Iraqi ground and hold it. Petraeus set up a system of substations instead of camps, where troops would enter and take a piece of ground (neighborhood or area of a city) and live there. These substations allowed our troops to keep the ground we had gained and didn't allow the enemy to creep back in.

And it worked. Our troops were embedded into hundreds of Iraqi communities and essentially policed their own neighborhoods. The enemy was forced to find ground unoccupied by the Americans, which became increasingly more difficult for them.

This crushed the insurgency. When Americans soldiers became part of a community and personally impacted the people around them, many of the enemy's supply routes, bomb-making facilities, and safe houses were destroyed. Our presence in the communities allowed interaction between the Iraqi people and us. This let us win their hearts and minds and achieve our strategic objectives.

Back when we retreated to safe zones and began making decisions for self-preservation purposes only, we lost our strategic edge. Our world of walls was our demise until the surge. After the surge, there were no walls—only free interaction between our forces and the Iraqi people. We pushed the bad guys out and shined the light of freedom into the lives of those under oppression. We thought our world of walls worked, but it was the enemy's strategy to immobilize us and make us fearfully ineffective.

Our World of Walls

Instead of the battlefields of Iraq, let's focus on our daily lives as Christians. The enemy recognizes the powerful impact your testimony has in the lives of unbelievers in your daily life. His goal, over the past several years in America, has been to challenge Christians with an environment that would make them lose their godly purpose and retreat to the safety of their world of walls for self-preservation. As Christians are retreating to a defensive posture from this world, the enemy has free reign over the hearts and minds of unbelievers. Without our light, the land grows darker and darker.

We need to remember that God is still in control and can shield us from the enemy's schemes. He doesn't need us to escape into our world of walls and depend on them for our protection. Rather, we need to trust Him while we remain open to touching the world. We have grown accustomed to living within the confines of our walls, and we can't see past them. Now the enemy has the church on its heels. He has pressed us into our world of walls and has now begun to attack us there.

Just like the insurgents in Iraq, our enemy is never satisfied with the victory he has gained. He wants it all. We haven't been on the offensive for some time and have allowed the spiritual insurgency to take over the land. This is a strategic failure of the body of Christ.

The enemy has also marked us as the enemy. Just as the insurgents polluted the minds of the Iraqis against the American forces, the devil perpetually poisons the minds of the world against the people of God. Something has to change and quickly if we are going to fulfill our role as the salt and light of this earth. In our case, no general in the land can refocus our strategy, but only the Commander of the Armies of the Most High God.

The church needs to surge! We need to tear down the walls separating us from our part of the world and begin taking ground and keeping it. Every time we leave the house without making some impact for the Lord, we have just lost that ground. Or conversely, we may never have gained it. We need to recognize our impact and calling and engage those around us for the Kingdom of God.

Imagine if I had not stood up for the Gospel in my office when my co-worker John tried to shut me up. I would have lost that strategic ground that God later used to spread the Gospel to many students and instructors. No one in that office ever challenged me again when it came to the Gospel. The enemy knows the potential of our impact on those around us and would like nothing more than to keep the Gospel locked in a concrete maze where it is no longer a threatening force. Whether it is behind the walls of our house, in our cubicle at work, or on the grounds of our church, many of us have retreated to a defensive posture that has paralyzed us.

You see, these methods, when used in the literal sense to defend and protect us from enemy attacks or natural disasters, are somewhat effective, but they have the opposite effect on Christ's impact on this world. The devil has convinced us that we need these walls to protect our family and ourselves, but after a while, they act as a prison, confining us to our own little world where we neither affect others nor are affected.

We have also prematurely withdrawn from Christian obligation to stand and fight for our land. We have adopted a mentality that the world is going to hell and we are ready for Jesus to return. We have given up on this world and on the mission God Himself gave us: to spread the Gospel. We have a battle on our hands, but we do not fight it the way the world does. Let me remind us all that Paul agreed we should stand up for Christ when he declared:

> *The weapons we fight with are not the weapons of the world. On the contrary, they have divine power to demolish strongholds. We demolish arguments and every pretention that sets itself up against the knowledge of God, and we take captive every thought to make it obedient to Christ* (2 Corinthians 10:4-5).

Political correctness, fear, distraction, selfishness, unwillingness, and self-preservation are some of the reasons our witness has been minimized. Our impact on the world around us is being contained and minimized by the walls we use to contain attacks or disasters.

I believe I had to go to Iraq to understand a world of literal walls before I could understand the spiritual walls that separate us from the world. In America, there are no fourteen-foot high concrete walls separating us from our coworker next to us. But that cubicle wall has become a T-wall in the office spaces of our lives, separating the believer from those who desperately need the message of Christ. There are also no T-walls separating us from our next-door neighbors. Imaginary property lines contain us instead. Who would ever have thought that property lines and aluminum garage doors would become T-walls containing us and our impact to the limits of the interior of our own homes?

The enemy frequently tried to silence the Apostle Paul or minimize his ministry's impact on those around him. Sometimes he did it through persecution and sometimes through pressure of society around him. The final time was through people in authority who attempted to use prison walls to contain him. Paul never allowed any of these things to silence his testimony, as he was "not ashamed of the Gospel, because it is the power of God for the salvation of everyone who believes" (Romans 1:16). The more determined the enemy became to silence Paul, the more determined Paul was at fulfilling his mission. No matter the obstacle, Paul never surrendered.

Surge, Church, Surge!

The devil knows the great impact we can make when we go on the offensive, entering the lives of others and tearing down spiritual strongholds. He has attempted to scare us into neglecting to share the Gospel, reach out, have compassion, meet the needs of our community, and show the love of God to the world around us.

In the workplace, Satan has tried to silence our message with laws and policies that allow every kind of filth and worldly point of view but eliminate the things of God by labeling them as offensive or proselytizing. I can tell you from first-hand experience that I have witnessed to many people in the workplace and have been successful. I have never been reprimanded, but I have been commended. If I can witness to criminals who just committed the most heinous of crimes, you can enter the life of the quiet co-worker in cubicle 3C. We can also step into the life of our next-door neighbor or the parents of our kid's classmates or whomever we encounter.

Get out, meet people, open up, live like people of freedom, stretch yourself and your personality. God didn't make us to be wimps who retreat. He made people who are more than conquerors. If we as Christians don't begin to surge in our world and take ground for the Kingdom of God, the enemy will (and has). The place where you live, work, attend school, or hang out is the substation you have been assigned to by the Almighty Strategist and General of the Armies of the Living God, Jesus Christ. You see, the people of God need to embrace the city block, school, or community they have been placed in and win the hearts and minds of the people around them for the Lord. God has already strategically embedded you in the area where he needs you. Stay connected and on the offense. Do not retreat to your world of walls.

God was the first to develop this type of warfare through evangelism. Through the numerous passages in the Word of God that call for Christians to proclaim the Gospel boldly, God is essentially ordering us to surge. If we all surged in our local situations, we could begin to take ground (souls) for the Kingdom and fulfill a major calling of God in our lives: to help others find the light switch! Let's turn this thing around and transform a seeming defeat into a surge of God before He returns. *Surge, Church . . . Surge!*

10

The Personal Mission Field

When I moved to Arizona, a young guy named Bobby lived across the street. He and his wife seemed like good people, but they were far from God. Bobby and I occasionally talked in the front yard, and I subtly mentioned the Gospel to him because I wasn't sure he would receive it. As time went by, I saw the need to be more than an acquaintance to him. After four years of living across the street from Bobby, I began making it a point to build a relationship with him. Only then did God open the door for the Gospel.

One evening, Bobby came over to ask my advice about a personal issue. I gave him the best advice I could, but then (because a relationship had been established through being neighbors) I asked him, "Bobby, when are you going to surrender your life to the Lord?"

He said that God had been calling him since the previous year when his marriage had almost fallen apart. One night several months prior, he and his wife, DeAnna, had a fight, and he stormed out to go for a walk. He asked God to show him an open door, and when he walked past my house, our door was wide open and we were having a large Bible study. He realized God was leading him, but he didn't receive it until I confronted him with the Gospel through our relationship.

I will never forget that night. As I shared the Gospel, Bobby began to weep. He poured his heart out to God and surrendered his life right there in my living room. Since then, Bobby and DeAnna have served the Lord with all their hearts and won many to the Lord. It was about relationship first, then the Gospel.

One of the greatest ways we can advance the Kingdom is by first reaching the people with whom we have some level of relationship. This realm of relationship and interaction has been divinely orchestrated in the life of the believer. It has great value, and we should take advantage of it. God has placed you in a strategic substation and given you an area to take and influence for the Kingdom. Instead of policing it, you are to make an impact on it with the Gospel. You are to show the love of God and spread His Gospel to those in your sphere of daily influence. I call this the personal mission field. It consists of family, friends, neighbors, co-workers/classmates, and people we meet by chance.

Evangelism through already existing relationships was the primary method of the early Christians in spreading the Gospel. The birth of the Church was due to the coming of the Spirit at Pentecost, but its continued growth was due to the Spirit working through believers in their daily lives to evangelize those around them. This was done primarily through the   (Greek for "oikos" in English), which was the house or household of those in that time period. Thomas Wolf, in his article entitled "Oikos Evangelism," states that the οικος was "the fundamental and natural unit of society, and consisted of one's sphere of influence—his family, friends, and associates. And equally important, the early church spread through oikoses—circles of influence and association." Through the οικος, Christians shared the Gospel with those closest to them. Through relationships, they changed the world.

Believers are called to be witnesses, but many may not know where to start. Remember, Jesus was clear that we need to be His witnesses in "Jerusalem, and in all Judea and Samaria, and to the ends of the earth" (Acts 1:8). When He said this to the disciples, they were already in Jerusalem, which was the first place He told them they would witness. So, allow me to paraphrase what Christ was saying:

> You are called to share the Gospel everywhere your foot touches, including where you are currently, where you travel, and wherever I may lead you in this world.

Too often, Christians focus only on the ends-of-the-earth portion of their mission field by giving to foreign missions through their local church. It's great to give to foreign missions, but what about all the other areas He was talking about? What about your hometown and the big city closest to you where you take your family on special occasions? We have forgotten and forsaken the majority of our calling. The ends of the earth are the places where we will probably spend the least amount of time, unless we are missionaries. God has orchestrated the lives of believers, and there is a plentiful harvest near our own homes.

The harvest is plentiful but the workers are few. Ask the Lord of the harvest, therefore, to send out workers into his harvest field (Matthew 9:37-38).

We cannot pray for the fulfillment of this scripture if we aren't willing to take part in the work. This work can begin in the life of every believer without taking a mission trip or doing inner-city street preaching with a church group. We can begin by ministering to those in the circle of people God has placed in our lives—our personal mission field. If we are going to surge, we must recognize that our personal situation in life is our mission field and surge there first.

This type of evangelism is sometimes called relational evangelism. Douglas Cecil, in his book entitled *The 7 Principles of an Evangelistic Life,* defines relational evangelism as "a place where the Gospel is shared as a natural result of the relationship that has developed over a period of time." Evangelizing where some level of relationship already exists is ideal for sharing the Gospel, as commonalities exist and the basic terms of the relationship have already been established. Cecil says that "out of our personal relationship with Jesus Christ flows our relationship with others and our relationship with the world."

This relational method of sharing the Gospel is a part of the Christian life. We should continually be developing new relationships and caring for those relationships with the love that permeates the Gospel. Since relationships already exist in our personal mission field, we should follow the advice of the Apostle Paul, who instructed the Christians in Ephesus that they should be "making the most of every opportunity, because the days are evil" (Ephesians 5:16). Your family, friends, neighbors, co-workers, classmates for students, and people you meet by chance account for most of the encounters you have during the course of your normal day or week. This list also begins with those in closest relationship with you. In Dawson's book *The Complete Evangelism Guidebook*, he calls these people the "ordinary people" we should be reaching with the Gospel.

Generally, your mission field consists of about ten to twenty people you interact with in the course of your daily life. You may be thinking, "What about my doctor, banker, and mailman?" These easily fit into the chance meetings group, since at one point you met them by chance. They are a subgroup called acquaintances. You may also be thinking, "How far in depth do I need to go?" or "I have a large extended family and many co-workers." Start small, where the closest relationship exists, and go from there.

Just as soldiers in Iraq were assigned a substation and were responsible for it, you are responsible for yours. Soldiers assigned to a neighborhood in Baghdad could never reach those in another neighborhood because they never encountered them. You are the only one who can encounter all those in your mission field. The pastor and other Christians cannot reach everyone in your town. They do not live where you live or work where you work, and they are certainly not related to your family. You are involved in all the areas that make up your assigned mission field.

I find it fascinating that research substantiates the vital need for the personal mission field. In 2009, Lynn Cathy wrote an excellent article called "Southern Baptists Urge Their Members to Evangelize More," which was published in *USA Today*. In it, Cathy stated that Lifeway Research surveyed over fifteen thousand people and "found only two ways most people said they were somewhat or very willing to 're-ceive information' about Jesus: 63% would hear it in a 'per-sonal conversation with a family member,' or with a friend or neighbor from the church (56%)." We can assume that these fifteen thousand people are a pretty good cross section of our society and seem, in a large percentage, to be open to hearing the Gospel from those closest to them.

Doesn't this sound very similar to the οικος (household) of the early church? The closest relationships (family) have the greatest potential for receptiveness to the Gospel, but the receptiveness decreases as the level of relationship decreases (friends and neighbors). I would assume this same trend in receptiveness continues to decrease as the level of relationship continues to decrease even further (co-workers, classmates, and chance meetings). That's why it's so important that we build relationships with those who are further away from us relationally. The closer the relationship, the more willing they are to receive the Gospel.

Implications of Embracing
Our Personal Mission Field

There is great potential for successful conversions and effective discipleship when Christians embrace their personal mission field. As believers witness to those closest to them, where a relationship already exists, the foundation for effective discipleship has already been laid. No longer will converts lose touch with those who led them to Christ. Instead, they will likely continue the familial relationship or friendship long after conversion. This continual relationship can provide the new Christian with the spiritual support system needed to grow in relationship with God.

This is vital as Christ called us to "go and make *disciples* of all nations" (Matthew 28:19), not just converts. One of the greatest problems in reaching the lost is that few people who surrender to God end up serving God. This may be due to a lack of full surrender but also may be due to the lack of discipleship to follow the encounter. So when you win someone to the Lord, your job is not complete; it has only begun. We will discuss this more later when we address the evangelism encounter.

Allow me to begin making this seem more personal to you. Wherever you are at this moment, close your mind's eye and consider each group of your mission field for a few moments and reflect on those people who make up that group in your life. Try to think about their faces, names, situations, and openness toward the things of God. This will give you a tangible understanding of those you have the great honor of impacting for the Kingdom of God. As you go throughout your week, try to focus on those in your mission field and begin to pray for the burden to reach each one of them and introduce them to your Savior. As you read on, try to fit the people in your life into these groups, and maybe you'll see those in your mission field more clearly and learn new ways to reach them.

If each Christian began sharing the Gospel with the few people in their personal mission field, we could add to the church greater numbers of converts than history has ever recorded. For example, if each Christian in America won a single soul, the Kingdom of God would grow by the millions of souls immediately. Then, if those who were won to the Lord were properly discipled, the number of true disciples would increase, and the church would grow exponentially!

Nehemiah and the Walls of God

The concept of taking initiative where God has placed you is nothing new in Christianity. In Nehemiah's day, the task was not to win souls but to rebuild the city walls of Jerusalem. He led this major undertaking with a few skilled workers, priests, noblemen, merchants, and commoners. The laborers were from all realms of social status, but all were called to the common task of rebuilding the wall.

More important, each of the workers took initiative and worked on the portion of the wall nearest his home or place of business. Commoners worked on the wall near their neighborhood, and the merchants worked on the portion of the wall nearest the marketplace. Each of them did the work of God where they spent their time on a daily basis. That was where they were familiar and knew the landscape better than anyone, so it seemed most appropriate to work on the wall there. With this strategy, they got that wall built.

The evangelism mission field is no different. Christians all have different specific purposes in life, but we all have the same general calling: to win souls. Just like those of Nehemiah's day, Christians are all called to the same common task of building the Kingdom of God. We should fulfill this calling in the places we go on a daily basis. We should work on this task where we live, work, and spend large amounts of time. The people of Nehemiah's day took initiative and pulled their own weight by laying brick where God had placed them. No one else was going to finish the work in their area, and neither can we expect others to pick up our slack in our personal sphere of influence.

Just as I had to take the initiative in my neighborhood to build a relationship with Bobby, we all need to recognize these opportunities in our local situations. The place in life God has assigned you is your personal responsibility—and a great opportunity. You are familiar with the people there. You know your family, friends, neighbors, co-workers, and class-mates better than you know anyone else and can make an im-pact on them. You know the landscape better than anyone there. You are called to that section of the wall, but instead of adding bricks, you are adding souls. Let prayer be your work plan, the people be the bricks, you be the builder, and let Christ be the mortar that holds it all together. Point them to the light switch, and let's get that wall done!

11

The Encounter

In January 2009, amidst an economic downturn and without any other options, I took a contract job as an interrogator for the Department of Defense (DOD). The DOD required all interrogators to attend a course at Fort Huachuca, Arizona, prior to their contracted deployment to Iraq. As a former Army CID agent, I was well versed in the art of criminal interrogation. Now I had been hired to conduct interrogations for Military Intelligence to gain information for a different purpose. As I proceeded through the course, the Lord began speaking to my heart that my purpose at Fort Huachuca was greater than merely becoming a better interrogator.

About six weeks into the course, my wife, Melissa, took me to lunch and told me that she had just read an e-mail I had received from my company. The e-mail informed me that many of the contract interrogator positions had been lost, and that I might not deploy to Iraq after all. I immediately asked the Lord, "Why did you send me here to exert all this effort if I were never meant to go to Iraq in the first place?" God answered me that very second and said, "Look at it another way." Immediately my spirit knew what God was trying to tell me.

The method I was being taught to interact with detainees mirrored the method I had been using for years to win souls. This school simply helped me better articulate what I had been doing as a personal evangelist. The process of interacting with others is not specific to interrogation, sales, or marketing but is basic to human nature.

God had a plan for me to equip believers in the art of soul winning, and this was His way of teaching me how to put it into words. That day, He called me to write this book, and I pray that through it you will gain the understanding of what makes a successful relationship that will provide fertile ground for the planting of the Gospel.

When my instructors taught me the phases of an interrogation, I knew they were common to any human interaction. They taught us to build rapport with the detainee, assess the detainee to determine what makes him tick and his current level of cooperation, develop an approach strategy based on the assessment, recognize the point at which the detainee is willing to cooperate, and then exploit him for the information he has.

These phases are basic to human interaction. Before people open their hearts to true conversation, rapport must be established. Building rapport is the first step in tearing down walls of defense and creating common ground that is suitable for conversation. Before we know we can trust people enough to go further in a relationship, we assess them by the things they say and what seems to drive them. Then we base the relationship on those terms to relate to them in ways that are compatible.

Let's take this a step further. We can use these phases to help us organize the evangelism encounter in our minds. Before people will open up about who they are, we first must build friendly terms of conversation. Then we have to get to know them in order to determine what direction they are going in life and what drives them. Next, based on that information, we can determine how we can deliver the Gospel in a way that speaks to their heart and situation. Then, if we are fortunate enough to see them receive the Gospel, we can recognize that point by their words and actions and lead them to salvation.

I have been reaching people all over the world for many years, using this basic method of dealing with people. My purpose in this has nothing to do with interrogation or the presentation of a worldly scheme to "sell" something. Nor am I insisting that we replace our God-given discernment with a five-step process of human origin. On the other hand, the way God made us to communicate with each other has been taught in many secular fields, but it is also useful in interacting with people for God. Our job is to recognize how we can use this knowledge for more effective encounters with unbelievers.

On the next page is a chart that may help you visualize all of the phases of the encounter.

Discernment of the Holy Spirit

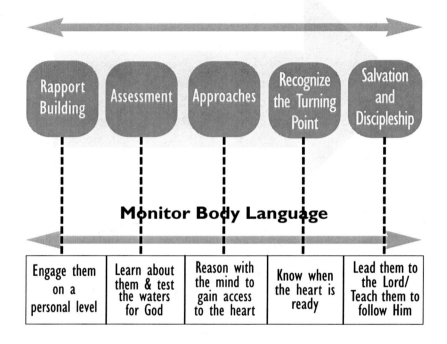

Rapport Building	Assessment	Approaches	Recognize the Turning Point	Salvation and Discipleship
Engage them on a personal level	Learn about them & test the waters for God	Reason with the mind to gain access to the heart	Know when the heart is ready	Lead them to the Lord/ Teach them to follow Him

Monitor Body Language

Allow me to describe to you a real encounter in which I used these basics of conversation and relationship to share the Gospel. Take for instance a chance meeting I had with some teenagers. In this case, I built rapport, assessed what made the unbelievers "tick," and then presented the Gospel.

On Saint Patrick's Day, 2010, I took my family to the park in our town of Sierra Vista, Arizona. After about ten rounds of "chase me, Daddy," I decided to take a break and sit down. I had my eye on a group of four teenagers, one of them playing classical guitar. They were seated and comfortable, which was where I wanted to be. I knew I could at least strike up a conversation with them, so I went and sat down with them as if I knew them personally. The guitarist was serenading two girls and another young man with songs like "Dust in the Wind" and "Wanted, Dead or Alive." I began to sing along with the guitar, and the group warmed up to me real quick. I then began asking each of them a few things about themselves. I didn't ask them their names but referred to them by what they were wearing or doing.

I called one of the girls "Cell Phone girl," the guitarist "Guitar Man," the other girl "Red-shirt Girl," and the other guy "Dude." I used these pet names every time I asked them a question and, without fail, they all snickered. This kept them loose and maintained rapport. After getting to know a little bit about each one, I asked about Guitar Man's shirt. It said *forgiven* on it and had a heart with a crown of thorns around it. I asked him what that meant.

"I got the shirt a long time ago," he said. "I don't know what it's about."

"I know exactly what it means." I acted as if I were trying to decipher the shirt's message and pointed to each part of the graphics as I explained them. "They're trying to portray Jesus Christ on your shirt. The crown of thorns was on His head, and then He died of a broken heart. The word 'Forgiven' is written below it because through Jesus, we are forgiven."

The group began to respond positively and open up a little. I took full advantage of this. "Do any of you believe in Jesus Christ?"

"I have my own beliefs," Guitar Man said, which was a macho contradiction to the message his shirt presented.

"Each person has been given a measure of faith to know that Jesus Christ is Lord, and that He came to this world and rocked it so hard that the calendars flipped upside down and time started over again," I said.

I noticed that Guitar Man and Cell Phone Girl had hearts in their eyes for each other. "Guitar Man, do you love Cell Phone Girl?"

He did. I then asked him if he had the choice to love other girls, and he said yes.

"Even though you could love other girls, you've chosen to love Cell Phone Girl. The same is true in our choice to serve

God or not." Then I popped the question. "Which of you is willing to stand up for Jesus Christ—the One who hung and died on a cross for you?"

Dude stood and said, "I'd like to go in that direction."

I put my hand on his shoulder, and he began to sob so profusely that he took off his shoe and sock and blew his nose on the sock. It was one of the most unique responses I had ever seen.

After Dude (whose name is Kyle) composed himself, I asked him, "God is calling. What is your answer?"

Kyle responded with an emphatic "Yes!"

The others were in shock as I led Kyle to salvation right there in the middle of the park's playground. Kyle was so broken, he could hardly keep it together. He thanked me over and over for taking the time to stop and see his need.

As I walked away from the group and on to meet my wife and daughters, I looked back. The group was all hugging each other and talking. Kyle explained to me later that his girl-friend had just dumped him, and he needed the love of God to heal his wounds.

Rapport

Did you notice that I began my encounter with Kyle and his friends by building rapport with them and gaining their trust? Rapport is the single most vital part of dealing with

anyone on a personal level. The ability to connect with an unbeliever and keep conversation alive is paramount to the encounter's success. Some people have to learn this trait because
they may not have been born with the gift of gab. But for most,
it is rather natural to participate and contribute to a conversation. And since most of the people you will be witnessing to are
people you already know, rapport building shouldn't be difficult. It will come in handy for those chance meetings.

All instances of witnessing require an element of rapport,
which is simply common ground where polite and friendly
exchanges can be made without fear. Rapport, in the case of
soul winning, is almost synonymous with trust. When
dealing with Kyle and his friends, I met them on a personal
level and engaged them in the things that were important to
them. I established common ground between us in those
songs we sang, which helped tear down the walls of defense
and build bonds of trust. The teenagers saw me as a genuinely friendly person who was interested in their lives.

Assessing

Initially, the focus of an encounter with an unbeliever is
getting them on conversational terms by building rapport.
Next, the Christian needs to assess the unbeliever for factors
that will affect the outcome of the entire process. These factors include the unbeliever's willingness to continue in conversation, his sentiment toward God, and what makes him
tick. When we know the answers to these questions, we can
make good decisions to plant a seed of the Gospel, water fertile ground, or possibly harvest a soul.

When talking with Kyle and his friends, I knew by the way they received my words that they were willing to continue in conversation, but I was unsure about their openness to the things of God. I introduced spiritual conversation to test the waters of their hearts and determine their openness or resistance to the Gospel. I did this through trying to decipher the message on the shirt Guitar Man was wearing. I used that to bring up God in conversation. From their responses to this discussion, I knew they were open and willing to hear more about God.

Approaches

Through assessing the teenagers, I also gained valuable insight into possible ways to present the Gospel. These are called approaches. Approaches are ways to relate the Gospel to unbelievers' lives through determining what makes them tick. The approach is the climax of the soul-winning encounter. It has the potential to turn the heart of the unbeliever toward God. Approaches are like little sermons or sermonettes. The approach is what the Gospel is packaged in and brings the Gospel to unbelievers in a way they can understand and also in a way that directly relates to their current situation. This is when we reason with the mind to gain access to the heart.

In the case of Kyle and his friends, my sermonette was focused on each person's measure of faith. I gave them confidence in Christ's Lordship by stating that He was so powerful that He caused time to start over again at His birth. I then followed up by relating the Gospel to their current situation and used their puppy love as a package for it. Little did I know that Kyle was the one this approach meant the most to, as he had just been dumped by his girlfriend. Do you see the Holy Spirit at work here? Through these approaches, I reasoned with their minds and gained access to their hearts. Like Paul in Athens, I related the Gospel to their lives without compromising the Gospel.

Recognize the Turning Point

Once I presented an opportunity for them to speak up for the Lord, Kyle did. He was so broken that he could not contain himself. This fact, along with his demeanor, made it pretty obvious that he was ready to make a commitment to God. The turning point for an unbeliever is a moment of duality. It happens when the unbeliever's resistance to God is broken and also when his will is broken before the Lord. Regarding the condition of the heart that God desires, the Bible states:

> *The sacrifices of God are a broken spirit; a broken and contrite heart, O God, you will not despise* (Psalm 51:17).

When the unbeliever is broken before the Lord, he accepts the truth for what it is. He no longer argues or debates but accepts the fact that Christ is the only source of truth. This moment is internal, but there are external indicators that you can recognize and act upon. Most of the time when unbelievers reach the turning point, they are willing to accept Christ but may not know where to start. But if we, the soul-winners, recognize the turning point and take action, we'll most certainly harvest a soul for the Lord. From my personal experience, many people will make a false conversion at this point if we let them, but if we are actively in tune with the Holy Spirit, then our discernment will bear witness of their authenticity and sincerity. If all these things line up, go for it! If not, plant the seed and allow God to do the rest.

Do you see the power of genuinely caring enough to take the time to intervene in the life of an unbeliever and find a way to present the Gospel? If we follow the basics of human interaction by building trust, understanding what makes them tick, then using those things as an avenue for the Gospel, we will win many. If we are going to lead others to the same light switch we have found, we must be willing to relate to them on their own terms, build relationship from there, and look for opportunities to share the Gospel. The possibilities are endless as we take a leap of faith and walk through the dark hallways of this world, saving those who have stumbled in the darkness.

12

Salvation and Discipleship

In 2009, while visiting my in-laws in Greeley, Colorado, I took my daughter Elise to the mall so she could go to the play area. When I got settled on a bench nearby, a young couple sat near me so they could see their toddler better. I did not feel particularly talkative, but they began telling me about their little boy and how rough-and-tumble he was. They opened up about their son and their experiences as his parents. I asked if they were married, and they said they were common-law married and had been together four years.

The dad, Hugo, stepped away to talk to a friend, and the mother, Victoria, mentioned that they had been through tough times in their relationship.

"I've been married a long time and have a peaceful marriage," I said, "but my wife and I both have the Lord in our lives. That makes a world of difference."

Victoria said, "Kind of like that movie *Fireproof*."

I realized she had some knowledge of the Lord. Her father had become a Christian, she said, and she was excited for him. I immediately asked her what she was going to do in her decision for the Lord. She said she did not feel worthy and did not know enough about the Bible or how to come to God. I knew this was an important moment.

Hugo returned and after a few minutes of getting to know him, I asked them, "What would it take for both of you to give your lives to the Lord tonight?"

After asking me a couple of questions, they both told me they were ready to start living for the Lord.

I asked them both if they were ready to start following Jesus from that moment forward and all the days of their lives. They both quietly said, "Yes." I knelt right there in the mall play area in front of a bunch of people and led them to the Lord. They prayed with me, accepted Jesus, and departed victoriously. I gave them some simple Christian principles regarding church, Bible reading, and prayer, and they were on their way.

I recognized initially that Hugo and Victoria had been through desperate times and were close to a decision point for God. They were ready and nothing was holding them back, so I catapulted them to the foot of the cross by asking, "What would it take for you both to give your life to the Lord tonight?" If I had not been bold, they might have gone away and never experienced salvation.

The truly amazing part of this story is what God continued to do in it. A few days after my encounter with Hugo and Victoria, I went to Iraq as a contract interrogator. Upon arrival at my camp in Baghdad, I went to meet the chaplains to see if there was something I could do to help. I didn't find the two chaplains that day, but I met their assistants, one of them a woman named Jennifer. I began telling the story of my encounter with Hugo and Victoria, and the two chaplain's assistants seemed interested. I placed my hand on Jennifer's shoulder to demonstrate how I'd done that with Hugo. I explained that I asked the young parents in the Greeley mall, "What would it take for you both to give your life to the Lord tonight?" The two chaplain's assistants liked the story, but then we parted ways, and I went back to work.

A few months later, Jennifer approached me and told me she would soon return to the US and wanted to thank me for what I had done for her. I was confused and asked, "What did I do?"

She told me that when we met, she was not saved but had played the part for a couple of years because she understood church people. She said that when I put my hand on her shoulder and described what I had asked Hugo and Victoria, she felt as if the Lord was asking her at that moment, "Jennifer, what would it take for you to give your life to the Lord today?"

She said she got saved that night and now desired to become a missionary and needed a letter of recommendation from me. I wrote a letter to the missionary program, and she returned home victorious.

Salvation

In my encounter with Hugo and Victoria, I realized they were at the point of conversion, and I led them to salvation. I did not have a canned prayer or salvation formula. I simply led them to a biblical relationship with Christ. I asked them if they were ready to follow Jesus with their lives, and they were, so we prayed. Sometimes when we have a person willing to surrender his life, we have a hard time putting salvation into words. I have had this problem in the past.

I have won the hearts of many unbelievers and helped them to the point that they were ready to accept Christ, but I didn't have the right words to lead them in their personal decision for Him. Other times I thought I had it all together, but when the moment of salvation came, I fumbled over the words and made the situation awkward. Now, after all these years of soul winning, I have a simple solution that is biblical and effective. Ask them to make Jesus both their Savior and Lord. Ask them to make an eternal commitment to Christ in full surrender, and be willing to follow, obey, and proclaim Him.

On the other hand, if the person is not ready to surrender, encourage him in the Lord but do not feel any obligation to have him make a commitment. Words don't mean anything if the heart is not ready. I have led many people through a prayer of salvation, but some never truly intended to serve the Lord.

We live in a time when people want to have a Savior but not a Lord. They want forgiveness and deliverance from their problems, but they are not willing to surrender their life to the Lordship of Christ. If you lead people in this condition through a salvation prayer, it may do more harm than good. They may have a false conversion, which may give them a false sense of salvation, and they will see no need to surrender in the future. If it feels like you are pressuring the person or trying too hard to seal their salvation, maybe you should consider whether they desire Christ as much as you desire them to come to Christ. The only true salvation is in full surrender, which will manifest itself in brokenness.

Discipleship

I was able to win Hugo and Victoria to the Lord and then unwittingly won Jennifer's heart to Him as well. But I did not have an opportunity to disciple them because I never saw them again. That was because they were people I met by chance, and no room was left for discipleship. In cases like these, we have to trust God that He has a plan for someone else to encourage the new believer. But the great thing about the personal mission field is that it complements discipleship, since most of those you win to God will probably continue to be a part of your everyday life. This is a perfect opportunity to serve as a mentor to them—a concept also known as discipleship.

Discipleship is showing another how to walk with God. The new believer will have a lot of questions, will need a lot of guidance, and will need your prayers and encouragement through the beginnings of this new life. Once you've won them, lead them. The new believer will need your advice on the kind of church they should choose, the kind of Bible they should buy, and the kind of things they should or shouldn't be involved in as a Christian.

These are all things the soul-winner can help young Christians with. Remember to continue rapport and serve as an example but don't be afraid to be a little more direct now that they have accepted Christ. You don't have to use any more approaches, but you will need to continue to inspire new believers. Encourage them to get baptized and, if necessary, facilitate it. Encourage them to begin studying the Bible and buy them one if necessary.

Over the first few weeks of new believers' lives, remain in frequent contact and serve as a guide for anything they encounter. Encourage them to begin building memories with God and to increase their faith by trusting God and seeing His hand move in their lives. Additionally, it is important for new believers to know they are now led by the Spirit and should walk in the Spirit in their daily lives. Be sure to inform them of God's desire for us to obey Him in all things.

I always explain to new believers that every Christian stands on a three-legged stool of prayer, Bible study, and fellowship. If any one of those three legs were missing, the Christian would fall. If any of the three legs were shorter than the others, the Christian would not be balanced. I encourage them in these areas and challenge them to stay balanced as a Christian.

Once you have determined people want to make a commitment to God, don't feel you have to say all the right things, but simply lead them to a full surrender to their Savior, Jesus. You have led them to the light switch, and now it's time to allow them to turn it on by showing them what true, biblical Christianity is. Once you have won their soul, continue to shine your light into their lives and encourage them on their journey. One day, they will lead others to the light switch!

13

My Evangelism Experiment

Now that you have heard my heart and have taken the journey with me through this book, I want to share some findings from my own personal research and experiment. My final work in seminary was a thesis on the topic of personal evangelism. I recognized that many Christians do not fulfill the Great Commission, and even when they tried to witness, they were ineffective.

I made several hypotheses and tested them through an experiment at my local church. I believed I knew several of the reasons why Christians are not winning souls and decided to test them to see if I were right. I developed an evangelism-training course entitled *The Light Switch*, which was administered at the church that I helped pastor in Sierra Vista, Arizona. The following is a thesis excerpt that shows my findings. I hope you will see the value of this teaching and implement it at your local church and use the methods in your personal life of witnessing.

Findings

The corporate church overwhelmingly accepts the scriptural mandate to evangelize, but very few Christians actively share their faith with those around them. Christians are private, not outspoken about their faith. They are not actively evangelizing but infrequently and passively provide a lesser form of spiritual encouragement to those around them, which falls desperately short of God's will.

I proposed that the lack of active, frequent, and effective evangelism was due to several factors, including misconceptions about biblical evangelism, false restrictions placed on evangelism, lack of teaching of biblical models of evangelism at the local church, a failure to embrace the concept of the personal mission field, and a corporate failure to embrace the Great Commission as normative and applicable to individual Christianity. The research demonstrates that much of this is the case in Christianity and can be corrected through proper teaching and dependence on the Holy Spirit.

The Light Switch Program

Following my research, I conducted a small-scale experiment of my own for local verification of the issues I found in the corporate church. I administered the *The Light Switch* program to a test group at my local church. This test group was comprised of ten Christians who attend and volunteer at my local church. The participants completed a pre-course survey and the evangelism course, and then they agreed to share the Gospel with at least three people in the following weeks. After three weeks, I sent a post-course survey to each of the participants. They completed and returned them to me within three additional weeks.

The following is a summary of the findings of both surveys and an analysis thereof, which shows remarkable improvement in their evangelistic awareness, urgency, and effectiveness.

Pre-Course Survey Findings

The analysis of the pre-course survey revealed little previous formal evangelism training and a low rate of evangelism. Additionally, hindrances that were reported centered around three major issues: fear, inadequate knowledge, and personal discomfort. Upon initial analysis of the pre-course survey alone, it seemed the participants allowed trivial issues and personal desires to dictate their evangelism habits and take priority over God's commands to win the lost. The pre-course findings showed the evangelism habits of the group were passive at best and did not measure up to the Gospel mandate.

The group overwhelmingly agreed that all Christians are called to fulfill the Great Commission but had mixed reporting regarding whether the Gospel should be preached by words or by actions. Additionally, many of the participants failed to evangelize those closest to them in their personal mission field and seemed purposely to avoid sharing the Gospel with those in their circle of family and friends. Most noteworthy, though, are the responses to a survey question that asked the participants to describe what they hoped to gain from the course.

All the participants reported they would like to overcome their personal weaknesses in evangelism, which were a broad spectrum of issues including a lack of confidence, discomfort in evangelism, lack of knowledge, unfamiliarity with witnessing methods, and not having a close relationship with God. These responses show the virtuous hearts of the participants. Regardless of their personal weaknesses, they were willing to improve. Only one of the ten participants had ever won a soul to Christ, and only a few reported having even passive evangelism habits. My pre-course survey findings regarding current levels of evangelism were not numerical but were reasonably consistent with Lifeway Research findings in that the participants reported evangelism was occurring "sporadically, occasionally, or not at all." At this point in my research, I could reasonably affirm that I had a similar sample of the Christian population as those in the broad studies mentioned.

Post-Course Survey Findings

The post-course survey findings provided much validation for all of my four hypotheses. The participants reported having a changed perspective on evangelism, a new understanding of the biblical methods of evangelism, lower fear levels, higher confidence levels, and an empowerment that supersedes most of the former obstacles that hindered their evangelism efforts. Participants reported at least twenty evangelism encounters and provided a summary of the encounters in their post-course surveys. These encounters provided the true assessment of the success of the course. The encounters revealed that the participants had transitioned from passive or a lack of evangelism to active evangelism as a way of life.

The participants reported encounters with all areas of the personal mission field, ranging from a mother witnessing to her grown son to a man witnessing to the person who stopped to help when his car broke down. The reasons for these positive evangelism encounters are manifold. Many of the participants reported an extremely low level of confidence and understanding in the pre-course survey but now report newfound knowledge and understanding, clear insight, confidence, new perspective, and courage to fulfill the calling of God.

When asked if the course has caused them to witness more, 60 percent of participants reported they have witnessed more after the course than before, while some reported they are more equipped but are not actively evangelizing the way they would like to. These responses validate my fourth hypothesis: when Christians are trained that evangelism is normative and prescriptive, they will do it.

In my survey, I asked the participants which people group they were most comfortable evangelizing. In the pre-course survey, many reported a hesitation to witness to those closest to them and wanted to witness only to strangers. But in the post-course survey, they reported a newfound desire to witness to friends and family. It seems these participants have begun embracing this calling and will likely be most effective in reaching unbelievers in these areas because of the relationships that already exist.

Implications

The implications of failure to implement these findings are devastating to the future of the church. Christians must be taught to embrace the biblical models of evangelism as well as their personal mission field. We all need to see the Great Commission as a normal part of Christian life. Failure to do so will result in a dwindling church that lacks fruit and a dying world lost without the Gospel. These surveys, along with the broad research conducted by other Christian organizations, show we have both a desperate lack of evangelism and an ineffective church.

The participants in my research test group represent a microcosm of the larger Christian community. The survey showed that, prior to the course, they were fearful, ill-equipped, and powerless people of God in the area of evangelism. On a larger scale, the corporate church is probably in the same condition, having minimal impact on the world around them. Jesus is coming back for a glorious church much like the boldly empowered early church that risked everything to win a soul. We must change the culture of the Christian community from one of passivity to activity before it's too late.

The corporate church must begin to embrace biblical models like the Pauline paradigm as part of the normal Christian life. When Christians are taught that evangelism is a job only the Holy Spirit does, they miss their calling and fail to walk in one of the main purposes of the Holy Spirit baptism, which is empowerment for evangelism. Only the Holy Spirit makes us ambassadors who speak on behalf of God. But when we fail to pursue souls actively, over-relying on the Holy Spirit to do our job, we fail to operate in that same Spirit.

Jesus was clear that we need to share the Gospel wherever we are: at home, at work, and in the places where we operate in our daily lives. Failure to embrace the people in this small sphere of interaction and influence will be catastrophic to the Kingdom of God. Our friends, family, co-workers and those we encounter by chance have been issued to us as a ministry, and we are their minister. We already have a relationship with those with whom we have something in common, and that can become a simple springboard for the introduction of the Gospel. I pray you will partner with my research and commit yourself to seeking out the lost in the dark rooms of this life and lead them through the obstacles to the *light switch*.

> *Whoever turns a sinner from the error of his way will save him from death and cover over a multitude of sins* (James 5:20).

Epilogue: Your Mission Is Now!

My challenge to you, should you accept it, is to share the Gospel of Jesus Christ with at least three people in the next thirty days. This is the same challenge I gave to the members of my evangelism experiment and they flourished in their calling. It quickly developed into a lifestyle of personal evangelism for them.

If you don't start now, the urgency may dissipate, and you could miss one of your great purposes for being on earth. Make a commitment right now that you are the watchman, the ambassador, and you are the only one who can fulfill your mission to those God has given you.

Where do you start? Those closest to you are most willing to receive the Gospel from you because a relationship is already established. Maximize the value of that relationship and use it to launch your sharing the Gospel. Whether you have a relationship with an unbeliever or not, do your best to ensure there is proper rapport built before sharing the Gospel to reduce any resistance. Remember to attempt to relate the Gospel to their life in some way, showing them how vital it is to their situation.

Don't forget that it is okay to be passionate about the Gospel, and in some cases, to plead with people to open their eyes. You don't have to have all the answers, but as you share how God changed your life, they may desire the same in theirs. Don't fear the outcome, but take a risk for God and step into the lives of those who are lost. And finally, whether you are led to plant a seed, water one already planted, or harvest the crop, allow God's power to work in you as you lead others to the *Light Switch!*

Bibliography

Abraham, William J. 1989. *The Logic of Evangelism.* Grand Rapids: William B. Eerdmans Publishing Co. http://books.google.com/books?id=ogoKN5nujK4C& print sec=frontcover&source=gbs_ge_summary_r&cad=0#v=onepa ge&q&f=false (accessed February 11, 2013).

Bottoms, Scott T. 2011. *Restoring the Centrality of the Spirit's Empowerment For Carrying Out the Great Commission: A Course to Equip Christians at Journey Church in the Process of the Evangelism.* DMin diss., Assemblies of God Theological Seminary.

Bruce, F.F. 1942. *The Speeches in the Acts of the Apostles.* http://www.biblicalstudies.org.uk/pdf/ speeches_bruce.pdf (accessed August 5, 2013).

Cathy, Lynn G. "Southern Baptists Urge Their Members to Evangelize More." USA Today (n.d.) http://usatoday30.us-atoday.com/news/religion/2009-03-25-baptist-evangelize_ N.htm (accessed February 12, 2013).

Cecil, Douglas M. 2003. *The 7 Principles of an Evangelistic Life.* Chicago: Moody Publishers. http://books.google.com/books?id=W7yzvRbtIDIC&printse c=frontcover&source=gbs_ge_summary_r&cad=0#v=onepage &q&f=false (accessed February 11, 2013).

Detrick, Don. 2007. "The Holy Spirit and Evangelism." *Enrichment Journal.* http://enrichmentjournal.ag.org/200802/ 200802_000_HS_Evangelism.cfm (accessed July 25, 2013).

Dobbins, Gaines Stanley. 1948. *Denominational Evangelism and Training the Laity.* Review and Expositor 45, no. 2: 183-192. ATLA Religion Database with ATLASerials, EBSCOhost (accessed July 21, 2013).

Palau, Luis. 1997. *The Church's Forgotten No. 1 Priority.* Enrichment Journal, Fall 1997. http://enrichmentjournal.ag.org/199704/ index.cfm (accessed February 12, 2013).

The Barna Group. 2005. "Survey Shows How Christians Share Their Faith." http://www.barna.org/ barna-update/article/5-barna-update/186-survey-shows-how-christians-share-their-faith. (Accessed February 12, 2013).

Wilke, John D. 2012. *Churchgoers Believe in Sharing Their Faith, Most Never Do.* http://www.lifeway.com/Article/research-survey-sharing-christ-2012 (Accessed 15 July, 2013).

Witherington, Ben III. 1998. *The Acts of the Apostles: A Socio-Rhetorical Commentary.* Grand Rapids: William B. Eerdmans Publishing Company.

Wolf, Thomas A. 1978. "Oikos Evangelism." *Church Growth: America.* 1978: 11. http://gracefamilyinfo.org/attachments/OikosEvangelism.pd f (accessed February 11, 2013)

About the Author

Evangelist and Author James Moore has lived an extraordinary life, but it has been in the ordinary situations in his life that he has made the greatest impact for God. James has used every situation in life to touch the lives of those around him and introduce the lost of this world to the Savior. He is a minister who believes that all Christians are fellow ministers of the Gospel to others in their daily lives.

His ministry has taken many forms from searching for Osama bin Laden in the mountains of Afghanistan to serving as a bodyguard for Secretary of Defense Donald Rumsfeld. No matter where God has taken him, he has been determined to win souls. His passion for evangelism and experiences have built him into a mighty leader with a desire to lead others to fulfill their calling as a witness for Jesus Christ. James lives in southern Arizona with his wife and two daughters.

To contact the author
and find more information on how to witness,
visit his website:
www.lightswitchbook.com